THE MINIMALISTIC ENTREPRENEUR

EMPOWER YOUR INVESTMENTS WITH AN ENTREPRENEURIAL MINDSET

ADV VINAY M CHOUDHARY

To the bold dreamers and strategic thinkers,
who believe in the power of simplicity and focus
to achieve extraordinary success.

This book is dedicated to every entrepreneur
who dares to streamline,
to every investor who values clarity over complexity,
and to all those on the journey
to mastering the art of minimalistic investing.

May this guide inspire you to unlock your fullest potential
with purpose, precision, and persistence.

Contents

The Minimalistic Entrepreneur

Preface

In an increasingly complex and fast-paced world, the quest for financial freedom and a fulfilling life often feels like an uphill battle. We are bombarded with endless options, conflicting advice, and the pressure to achieve success quickly. Amid this noise, the concept of minimalism offers a refreshing perspective—one that emphasizes simplicity, intentionality, and a focus on what truly matters.

This book, The Minimalistic Entrepreneur: Investing in the Stock Market, was born out of my own journey to find a balance between financial success and a life of purpose. Like many, I once believed that the key to wealth was to chase every opportunity, diversify into countless ventures, and never stop moving. But as I navigated the ups and downs of the financial world, I realized that true success is not about accumulating more—it's about being intentional with less.

Minimalistic entrepreneurship is not about deprivation or austerity. It's about making smart, purposeful choices that align with your values and long-term goals. It's about investing in a way that is both simple and effective, allowing you to grow your wealth while enjoying the peace of mind that comes from knowing you are on the right path.

This book is designed to be a guide for anyone who seeks to take control of their financial future without getting lost in the complexities of modern investing. Whether you are just starting out or looking to refine your existing strategy, the principles and strategies outlined here will help you achieve financial independence with clarity and confidence.

Throughout these pages, you'll find practical advice on how to build and manage a diversified investment portfolio, navigate market cycles, and stay resilient in the face of uncertainty. You'll also discover the profound benefits of adopting a minimalist approach—not just in your financial life, but in every aspect of your journey as an entrepreneur and investor.

Writing this book has been a deeply personal endeavor. It reflects my own experiences, the lessons I've learned, and the insights I've gained from years of working in the financial industry. My hope is that it will inspire you to embrace a simpler, more focused approach to investing—one that empowers you to build lasting wealth while living a life that is rich in meaning and fulfillment.

As you embark on your journey as a Minimalistic Entrepreneur, remember that success is not a destination but a process. It's about making consistent, thoughtful decisions that move you closer to your goals, one step at a time. I encourage you to read this book with an open mind and a willingness to challenge conventional wisdom. The principles within these pages have the power to transform not just your financial life, but your overall sense of purpose and satisfaction.

Thank you for allowing me to be a part of your journey. I wish you every success as you apply the lessons of minimalistic entrepreneurship to create a future that is truly your own.

With best wishes,

Adv. Vinay M Choudhary

Acknowledgements

This book would not have been possible without the support, guidance, and inspiration from many individuals along the way.

First and foremost, I want to express my deepest gratitude to my family and friends, who have been my constant pillars of strength. Your unwavering support and belief in my vision have given me the drive to pursue this project to completion.

To the mentors and fellow entrepreneurs who shared their wisdom, thank you for teaching me the true value of focus, clarity, and simplicity in business and investing. Your insights have shaped not only this book but also my approach to life.

A heartfelt thanks to my readers and clients—your curiosity and passion for learning have been the fuel behind every word written here. Your desire to succeed with a minimalistic yet impactful approach to investing has inspired the content of this book.

Lastly, I want to acknowledge the ever-evolving world of entrepreneurship and investing. The lessons and experiences gained from navigating this journey have been the foundation of this book, and I am deeply grateful for the challenges and triumphs that have come my way.

To everyone who contributed to this book, directly or indirectly, my sincere thanks.

About The Author

Vinay M Choudhary is a seasoned advocate and legal expert with a deep passion for entrepreneurship, investing, and financial empowerment. Hailing from Thane, Maharashtra, India, Vinay's unique combination of legal acumen and entrepreneurial spirit has helped numerous clients navigate the complexities of business and financial strategies.

With years of experience in both the courtroom and the boardroom, Vinay's approach to investing is rooted in simplicity and focus—believing that less complexity often leads to greater success. His philosophy of minimalistic entrepreneurship is designed to empower investors by helping them make clearer, more impactful decisions in an often overwhelming financial world.

Through his work, Vinay has continuously emphasized the importance of strategic thinking, disciplined investing, and the pursuit of long-term goals. His insights have not only helped his clients succeed, but they have also inspired many to adopt a more thoughtful, purpose-driven approach to their financial futures.

When he's not advising clients or penning his next book, Vinay can be found exploring new investment strategies, mentoring aspiring entrepreneurs, and simplifying complex legal challenges into actionable solutions. The Minimalistic Entrepreneur is his latest contribution to the world of business and investing, offering readers a fresh perspective on building wealth with clarity, focus, and intention.

Prologue

In a world where complexity often masquerades as sophistication, the path to success can feel overwhelming. We are bombarded with an endless array of choices, strategies, and advice on how to invest, grow wealth, and build a business. Yet, buried beneath the noise lies a simple truth: true mastery comes not from doing more, but from doing what truly matters.

This book is born out of that realization. It is a guide for those who are ready to break free from the clutter and embrace a more focused, intentional approach to investing and entrepreneurship. A minimalist approach.

Minimalistic entrepreneurship is not about cutting corners or taking the easy way out. On the contrary, it requires discipline, clarity, and a deep understanding of what drives success. It's about identifying the core principles that work, eliminating distractions, and focusing your energy on the few actions that deliver the greatest impact.

In the pages that follow, you will discover the power of simplicity in investing—how a streamlined strategy can outperform even the most complex portfolios. You will learn how to cultivate the mindset of an entrepreneurial minimalist, someone who embraces focus, efficiency, and purpose in every decision. Most importantly, you will see how this approach can transform not only your investments but your life as a whole.

This book is not a traditional roadmap filled with complicated jargon and endless steps. It's a call to strip away the unnecessary and embrace the essentials. It's a guide for those who understand that less is often more—and who are ready to apply that principle to achieve financial independence and entrepreneurial success.

Welcome to the journey of the minimalistic entrepreneur. Your success starts here—with clarity, purpose, and focus.

Introduction

Imagine waking up one morning to find that your net worth has increased by thousands of dollars overnight. You haven't launched a new product, closed a big sale, or even left your bed. Welcome to the world of the Minimalistic Entrepreneur, where your money works tirelessly on your behalf, even while you sleep.

In the bustling cafes of Silicon Valley, the gleaming skyscrapers of Wall Street, and the garages-turned-workshops across the world, a familiar story of entrepreneurship has been told for decades. It's a tale of visionaries burning the midnight oil, of risk-takers mortgaging their homes to fund their dreams, of individuals sacrificing everything on the altar of innovation and success. We've been conditioned to believe that this high-stakes, all-or-nothing approach is the only path to entrepreneurial success.

But what if I told you there's another way? A way that allows you to participate in the exhilarating world of business ownership without sacrificing your peace of mind, your work-life balance, or your financial security. Welcome to the revolution of the Minimalistic Entrepreneur.

The Genesis of an Idea

The concept of the Minimalistic Entrepreneur was born out of a simple observation: in the modern economy, you don't need to build a business to own one. The stock market – that grand, sometimes intimidating, always exciting marketplace of company ownership – offers a backdoor to entrepreneurship that many have overlooked.

Think about it. When you buy stocks, you're not just making a bet on a company's future performance. You're buying a piece of that company. You become an owner, entitled to a share of its profits and growth. It's entrepreneurship, distilled to its purest form.

But why "minimalistic"? Because this approach strips away the complexities and demands of traditional entrepreneurship. No need to manage employees, grapple with supply chains, or lose sleep over cash flow. Your role is simple: invest wisely, then let the power of the market do the heavy lifting.

The Power of Passive Ownership

Picture two individuals: Alice and Bob. Alice is a traditional entrepreneur. She's poured her life savings into starting a boutique tech company. She works 80-hour weeks, juggles countless responsibilities, and lives with the constant stress of making payroll and satisfying investors.

Bob, on the other hand, is a Minimalistic Entrepreneur. He's invested in a diversified portfolio of stocks, including a stake in Alice's company. While Alice is burning the candle at both ends, Bob is free to pursue his passions, spend time with family, or even start other ventures. Yet, if Alice's company succeeds, Bob will reap the same relative rewards from his investment as Alice does from her grueling work.

This is the power of passive ownership. It's not about getting something for nothing – it's about leveraging the efforts and innovations of others to build your own wealth. It's about making your money work as hard as you do.

A New Paradigm for a New Era

We live in an age of unprecedented opportunity. The democratization of finance through online brokerages and fractional shares means that anyone with an internet connection and a few dollars can become a part-owner in some of the world's most successful companies. You no longer need millions to build a diverse, potentially lucrative portfolio.

This book is your roadmap to navigating this new landscape. We'll journey together from the basics of stock market investing to advanced strategies for building and managing your portfolio. We'll explore the mindset shift required to think like a Minimalistic Entrepreneur, and we'll delve into the lifestyle benefits that come with this approach.

You'll learn how to:
- Analyze companies like a seasoned investor
- Build a diversified portfolio that aligns with your goals
- Manage risk and maximize returns
- Leverage the power of compound interest to build lasting wealth
- Navigate market ups and downs with confidence
- Achieve financial freedom through passive income

Whether you're a college student looking to get a head start on building wealth, a busy professional seeking to diversify your income streams, or a retiree aiming to grow your nest egg, the Minimalistic Entrepreneur approach offers a path to financial growth and freedom that's accessible to everyone.

The Journey Ahead

As we embark on this journey together, I want you to imagine a future where your money works as hard as you do. A future where you have the freedom to pursue your passions, spend time with loved ones, and live life on your own terms, all while building substantial wealth.

This isn't a get-rich-quick scheme or a magic bullet. Becoming a successful Minimalistic Entrepreneur requires knowledge, patience, and discipline. But with the right tools and mindset, it's a path that's open to anyone willing to learn and take action.

So, are you ready to redefine what it means to be an entrepreneur? Are you prepared to leverage the power of the stock market to build lasting wealth and achieve true financial freedom? If so, turn the page, and let's begin your transformation into a Minimalistic Entrepreneur.

Your journey to financial empowerment starts now.

CHAPTER ONE

THE MINIMALISTIC ENTREPRENEUR DEFINED

Who is a Minimalistic Entrepreneur?

Picture this: It's a sunny Tuesday afternoon. While millions of people are hunched over their desks, eyes glued to computer screens, our protagonist, Sarah, is lounging in a hammock, sipping a freshly squeezed lemonade. Her smartphone pings - another dividend payment has just hit her account. Sarah smiles, knowing that her carefully chosen investments are hard at work, even as she enjoys her leisure time. This is the life of a Minimalistic Entrepreneur.

But who exactly is a Minimalistic Entrepreneur? Let's break it down.

A Minimalistic Entrepreneur is an individual who harnesses the power of the stock market to build wealth and achieve financial freedom, without the day-to-day demands of running a traditional business. They are investors who view their stock portfolio as their "business," and the companies they invest in as their "employees."

Key characteristics of a Minimalistic Entrepreneur include:

1. Ownership Mindset:

Unlike casual investors who may see stocks as mere numbers on a screen, Minimalistic Entrepreneurs understand that buying stocks means buying a piece of a real business. They think like owners, not speculators.

2. Passive Income Focus:

While they may have other sources of income, Minimalistic Entrepreneurs are committed to building streams of passive income through dividends and capital appreciation.

3. Long-term Perspective:

They understand that true wealth is built over time. Minimalistic Entrepreneurs are not swayed by get-rich-quick schemes or short-term market fluctuations.

4. Continuous Learning:

The stock market is dynamic, and so is the Minimalistic Entrepreneur. They are committed to ongoing education about investing, market trends, and economic factors that may affect their portfolio.

5. Risk-aware, Not Risk-averse:

While they seek to minimize unnecessary risks, Minimalistic Entrepreneurs understand that some level of risk is inherent in investing. They manage this risk through careful research and diversification.

6. Efficiency-oriented:

True to the "minimalistic" nature, they seek maximum results with minimum input. This doesn't mean they're lazy; rather, they're strategic about where they focus their time and energy.

7. Freedom-seekers:

Ultimately, Minimalistic Entrepreneurs are driven by the desire for financial freedom and the lifestyle flexibility it affords.

Let's consider our friend Sarah again. She spent years working in corporate finance, but always dreamed of having more control over her time and finances. Instead of starting a traditional business, Sarah educated herself about stock market investing. She began allocating a significant portion of her salary to carefully researched stock purchases.

Over time, Sarah's portfolio grew. She reinvested her dividends, took advantage of her company's stock purchase plan, and continuously expanded her knowledge of different sectors and investment strategies. After a decade, her dividend income matched her salary. Shortly after, she was able to leave her 9-to-5 job, achieving the freedom she had always desired.

Sarah's story illustrates the journey of a Minimalistic Entrepreneur. She didn't create a new product or service. She didn't manage employees or worry about operational challenges. Instead, she leveraged the power of ownership in existing businesses to create her own financial success story.

It's important to note that being a Minimalistic Entrepreneur doesn't mean you can't have a traditional job or start a conventional business if you wish. Many Minimalistic Entrepreneurs maintain careers they enjoy, using their investment income to supplement their earnings or accelerate their path to financial independence. Others use this approach as a stepping stone, building their investment income to a level that provides the security to start a more traditional business venture.

The beauty of the Minimalistic Entrepreneur approach lies in its flexibility. Whether you're looking to escape the 9-to-5 grind, supplement your existing income, or simply build long-term wealth, this strategy can be tailored to your individual goals and circumstances.

The Philosophy of Minimalistic Entrepreneurship

At its core, the philosophy of Minimalistic Entrepreneurship is about redefining success, freedom, and the very nature of business ownership. It's a mindset that challenges traditional notions of entrepreneurship and wealth-building, offering a path that aligns with the evolving values and realities of the 21st century.

Leveraging Existing Businesses

The first pillar of this philosophy is the idea of leveraging existing businesses. Traditional entrepreneurship often glorifies the creation of something new - a revolutionary product, a disruptive service, a never-before-seen business model. While there's certainly value in innovation, Minimalistic Entrepreneurship recognizes that there's also immense opportunity in becoming a part-owner of established, successful businesses.

Consider tech giant Apple, e-commerce behemoth Amazon, or consumer goods stalwart Procter & Gamble. These companies have teams of brilliant minds working tirelessly to innovate, expand, and increase shareholder value. As a Minimalistic Entrepreneur, you can benefit from their efforts simply by owning a piece of these companies through stock ownership.

This approach allows you to participate in the success of multiple businesses across various sectors, without the need to be an expert in each field or to manage the day-to-day operations. It's about working smarter, not harder.

Minimalism in Business Approach

The second pillar is the application of minimalist principles to business ownership. Minimalism, as a broader philosophy, is about focusing on what truly matters and eliminating the unnecessary. In the context of Minimalistic Entrepreneurship, this translates to stripping away the complexities often associated with traditional business ownership.

Gone are the worries about managing employees, dealing with suppliers, or staying on top of changing regulations. Your role as a Minimalistic Entrepreneur is focused solely on making informed investment decisions and managing your portfolio. This streamlined approach allows you to achieve business ownership's financial benefits without its often-overwhelming responsibilities.

The Power of Passive Income

The third pillar, and perhaps the most transformative, is the emphasis on passive income. In the traditional work model, income is directly tied to time spent working. You work an hour, you get paid for an hour. This model inherently limits your earning potential to the number of hours in a day.

Minimalistic Entrepreneurship breaks this link between time and money. Through carefully chosen stock investments, particularly in dividend-paying companies, you can create streams of income that flow whether you're working, sleeping, or sipping cocktails on a beach. This passive income is the key to true financial freedom.

Imagine waking up to find that you've earned money overnight, simply because companies you partially own have been hard at work while you slept. This isn't a fantasy - it's the everyday reality for successful Minimalistic Entrepreneurs.

Alignment with Modern Values

The philosophy of Minimalistic Entrepreneurship isn't just about money - it's about lifestyle design. It aligns perfectly with several key trends and values of our time:

1. Work-Life Balance:

By creating passive income streams, Minimalistic Entrepreneurship allows for a better balance between work and personal life. It gives you the freedom to pursue passions, spend time with loved ones, or travel the world, without sacrificing financial security.

2. Location Independence:

In an age of remote work and digital nomadism, Minimalistic Entrepreneurship offers the ultimate location independence. Your "business" can be managed from anywhere with an internet connection.

3. Sustainability:

Instead of constantly chasing growth and expansion, as many traditional businesses must, Minimalistic Entrepreneurship allows for a more sustainable approach to wealth building. It's about steady, long-term growth rather than the often unsustainable rapid scaling of traditional startups.

4. Democratization of Wealth:

With the rise of fractional shares and low-cost brokerages, Minimalistic Entrepreneurship is accessible to a wider range of people than ever before. It offers a path to wealth building that doesn't require large amounts of starting capital or specialized business knowledge.

5. Lifelong Learning:

The stock market is a reflection of our ever-changing world. As a Minimalistic Entrepreneur, you're encouraged to stay informed about global events, technological advancements, and economic trends. This aligns with the growing emphasis on lifelong learning in our knowledge-based economy.

A New Paradigm of Success

Perhaps most importantly, the philosophy of Minimalistic Entrepreneurship offers a new paradigm of success. In this paradigm, success isn't measured by the size of your company or the number of employees you manage. It's measured by the freedom you have to live life on your own terms.

Success, in the Minimalistic Entrepreneurship worldview, means having the financial security to say "no" to things that don't align with your values and "yes" to the experiences and opportunities that truly matter to you. It's about building wealth not for its own sake, but as a tool for creating the life you want to live.

This philosophy recognizes that in our complex, fast-paced world, true luxury is not about accumulating more - more responsibilities, more stress, more stuff. Instead, it's about having the freedom to choose how you spend your time and energy.

As we move forward in this book, we'll explore how to put this philosophy into practice. We'll delve into the practical steps of becoming a Minimalistic Entrepreneur, from developing the right mindset to making smart investment decisions. But throughout our journey, keep this philosophy in mind. It's not just about building wealth - it's about redefining what it means to be successful in the modern world.

Comparing Traditional Entrepreneurship and Minimalistic Entrepreneurship

To truly appreciate the unique advantages of the Minimalistic Entrepreneur approach, it's helpful to contrast it with traditional entrepreneurship. Both paths can lead to financial success and personal fulfillment, but they differ significantly in their methods, risks, and lifestyle implications. Let's break down these differences across several key dimensions.

1. Initial Capital Requirements

Traditional Entrepreneurship: Often requires significant upfront investment. Whether it's for product development, office space, inventory, or staff salaries, traditional entrepreneurs frequently need to raise substantial capital to get their ventures off the ground. This might involve dipping into personal savings, taking out loans, or seeking investors - all of which come with their own risks and pressures.

Minimalistic Entrepreneurship: Can start with as little as the cost of a single share of stock. With the advent of fractional shares, you can begin your journey as a Minimalistic Entrepreneur with just a few dollars. This low barrier to entry makes it accessible to a much wider range of people, regardless of their current financial situation.

2. Time Commitment

Traditional Entrepreneurship: Typically demands an enormous time investment, especially in the early stages. The phrase "24/7" is often used to describe the life of a startup founder. Weekends, holidays, and work-life balance can become foreign concepts as entrepreneurs pour their time and energy into getting their businesses off the ground.

Minimalistic Entrepreneurship: Allows for a much more flexible time commitment. While it does require time for research, analysis, and portfolio management, these activities can often be done on your own schedule. Once your investment strategy is in place, the day-to-day time requirement can be minimal.

3. Skill Set Required

Traditional Entrepreneurship: Demands a diverse range of skills. Entrepreneurs need to be jacks-of-all-trades, especially in the early stages of their businesses. They might find themselves acting as CEO, CFO, CMO, and janitor all in the same day. As the business grows, they need to develop leadership and management skills to effectively guide their team.

Minimalistic Entrepreneurship: Focuses on a more specific set of skills. While broad business knowledge is beneficial, the core skills revolve around financial literacy, market analysis, and investment strategy. These skills can be developed over time through study and practice, without the pressure of having to master every aspect of running a business.

4. Risk Profile

Traditional Entrepreneurship: Often involves high risk. The statistics on startup failure rates are sobering, with some estimates suggesting that up to 90% of new businesses fail. Entrepreneurs often put their personal finances, reputation, and career trajectory on the line when starting a new venture.

Minimalistic Entrepreneurship: Allows for more controlled risk management. While all investing involves some level of risk, Minimalistic Entrepreneurs can mitigate this through diversification, careful research, and long-term strategies. The risk of total loss, while still present, is generally lower than in traditional entrepreneurship.

5. Scalability

Traditional Entrepreneurship: Scalability often requires significant additional resources. Growing a traditional business typically means hiring more staff, expanding to new locations, or increasing production capacity - all of which require additional capital and introduce new complexities.

Minimalistic Entrepreneurship: Scales effortlessly. Whether you're investing $1,000 or $1,000,000, the fundamental process remains the same. Increasing your investments doesn't necessarily increase the complexity of managing them.

6. Income Generation Timeline

Traditional Entrepreneurship: Often involves a significant delay before seeing any income. Many businesses operate at a loss for months or even years before turning a profit. Entrepreneurs might go long periods without drawing a salary as they reinvest everything into growing the business.

Minimalistic Entrepreneurship: Can start generating income almost immediately, especially if focusing on dividend-paying stocks. While the income might start small, it can begin flowing from day one and grow steadily over time.

7. Exit Strategy

Traditional Entrepreneurship: Exit strategies often involve selling the business, going public, or passing it on to new management. These can be complex, time-consuming processes that may or may not result in the desired outcome.

Minimalistic Entrepreneurship: Offers simple and flexible exit options. Stocks can typically be sold quickly and easily if you need to access your capital. There's no need for complex legal processes or negotiations.

8. Impact of Economic Downturns

Traditional Entrepreneurship: Economic downturns can be existential threats to traditional businesses. A recession might dramatically reduce customer demand or dry up needed financing, potentially forcing the business to close.

Minimalistic Entrepreneurship: While not immune to economic downturns, a well-diversified portfolio can weather storms more easily. Market downturns can even present opportunities to invest at discounted prices.

9. Personal Brand and Identity

Traditional Entrepreneurship: Often involves building a personal brand closely tied to the business. Entrepreneurs frequently become the face of their companies, which can bring both opportunities and pressures.

Minimalistic Entrepreneurship: Allows for a separation between personal identity and investment activities. You can be a successful Minimalistic Entrepreneur without anyone knowing about your financial activities.

10. Innovation and Market Impact

Traditional Entrepreneurship: Often focuses on bringing new products, services, or business models to market. Successful traditional entrepreneurs can have a significant impact on their industries and society at large.

Minimalistic Entrepreneurship: While not directly innovating, Minimalistic Entrepreneurs support innovation by providing capital to innovative companies. They play a crucial role in the ecosystem by allocating resources to promising ventures.

The Hybrid Approach

It's worth noting that these approaches are not mutually exclusive. Many successful individuals incorporate elements of both traditional and Minimalistic Entrepreneurship in their wealth-building strategies. You might, for example, run a traditional business while also building a portfolio of stock investments. Or you might start as a Minimalistic Entrepreneur and use the capital and knowledge gained to launch a traditional venture later on.

The key is to understand the strengths and challenges of each approach and choose the path (or combination of paths) that best aligns with your goals, skills, and lifestyle preferences.

As we proceed through this book, we'll dive deeper into how you can leverage the unique advantages of Minimalistic Entrepreneurship to build wealth, create freedom, and achieve your financial goals. Whether you're looking for an alternative to traditional entrepreneurship or a complement to your existing business activities, the Minimalistic Entrepreneur approach offers a powerful toolkit for financial success in the modern world.

11

CHAPTER TWO

Becoming a Minimalistic Entrepreneur

Now that we've explored the concept and philosophy of Minimalistic Entrepreneurship, it's time to roll up our sleeves and dive into the practical aspects of embarking on this journey. Becoming a Minimalistic Entrepreneur is not just about buying some stocks and hoping for the best. It requires a shift in mindset, the development of key skills, and a clear vision of your financial goals. In this chapter, we'll explore these crucial elements that will set you on the path to success as a Minimalistic Entrepreneur.

Mindset Shift: From Active Business Owner to Passive Investor

The first step in becoming a Minimalistic Entrepreneur is to undergo a fundamental shift in how you think about business ownership and wealth creation. This mindset shift is crucial because it lays the foundation for everything that follows.

Embracing Passive Ownership

Traditional entrepreneurship often glorifies the "hands-on" approach - the idea that success comes from being deeply involved in every aspect of your business. As a Minimalistic Entrepreneur, you need to embrace a different paradigm: passive ownership.

This doesn't mean being completely detached or uninvolved. Rather, it means understanding that you can create value and build wealth without being in the driver's seat of day-to-day operations. Your role is that of a strategic investor, not an operational manager.

Consider the story of Michael, a former tech startup founder. Michael spent years working 80-hour weeks, dealing with the stress of payroll, client demands, and the constant pressure to innovate. While his company was moderately successful, he found himself burnt out and yearning for a change.

When Michael discovered the concept of Minimalistic Entrepreneurship, it was a revelation. He realized that he could leverage his business acumen and industry knowledge to identify promising companies to invest in, without the need to run these companies himself. Over time, he transitioned from being a stressed-out startup founder to a calm, collected investor with a diverse portfolio of tech stocks.

Michael's story illustrates the power of embracing passive ownership. By shifting his mindset, he was able to achieve his financial goals while reclaiming his time and reducing his stress levels.

Cultivating Patience and Long-Term Thinking

Another crucial aspect of the Minimalistic Entrepreneur mindset is the ability to think long-term. In the world of traditional entrepreneurship, there's often pressure for rapid growth and quick exits. As a Minimalistic Entrepreneur, you need to cultivate patience and embrace the power of compound growth over time.

This might mean holding onto stocks for years or even decades, reinvesting dividends, and resisting the urge to react to short-term market fluctuations. It's about understanding that true wealth is built gradually, not overnight.

Consider the approach of legendary investor Warren Buffett, often called the "Oracle of Omaha." Buffett is famous for his long-term investment strategy and his quote, "Our favorite holding period is forever." This patient, long-term approach has made him one of the wealthiest people in the world.

As a Minimalistic Entrepreneur, channel your inner Buffett. Cultivate the patience to hold onto high-quality investments through market ups and downs, always keeping your eyes on the long-term horizon.

Redefining Success

Becoming a Minimalistic Entrepreneur also involves redefining what success means to you. In traditional entrepreneurship, success is often measured by metrics like company size, market share, or exit valuations. As a Minimalistic Entrepreneur, your measures of success might look quite different.

Your success might be measured by:
- The stability and growth of your passive income streams
- The diversity and resilience of your investment portfolio
- The amount of free time you have to pursue your passions
- Your ability to weather financial storms without stress
- The peace of mind that comes from knowing your financial future is secure

Take a moment to reflect on what success means to you. How would your life look if you achieved "success" as a Minimalistic Entrepreneur? Visualizing this can be a powerful motivator as you embark on this journey.

Embracing Continuous Learning

The final key aspect of the Minimalistic Entrepreneur mindset is a commitment to continuous learning. The world of investing is vast and ever-changing. Markets evolve, new industries emerge, and global events can rapidly shift the economic landscape.

As a Minimalistic Entrepreneur, you need to cultivate a hunger for knowledge. This means staying informed about market trends, understanding economic indicators, and continuously refining your investment strategies.

But this learning extends beyond just financial knowledge. Successful Minimalistic Entrepreneurs are often voracious readers and learners across a wide range of subjects. They understand that knowledge from diverse fields can inform their investment decisions and help them spot opportunities that others might miss.

For example, an understanding of climate science might help you identify promising renewable energy stocks. Knowledge of demographic trends could inform investments in healthcare or real estate. A grasp of technological advancements might guide your investments in the tech sector.

Embrace this journey of lifelong learning. See it not as a chore, but as an exciting opportunity to constantly expand your understanding of the world and refine your skills as an investor.

Practical Steps for Mindset Shift

Shifting your mindset doesn't happen overnight. Here are some practical steps you can take to cultivate the Minimalistic Entrepreneur mindset:

1. Start a learning routine:

Dedicate time each day or week to reading about investing, market trends, and diverse subjects that interest you. This could be through books, financial news websites, podcasts, or online courses.

2. Practice patience:

Next time you make an investment, commit to holding it for a set period (say, one year) regardless of short-term price movements. This will help you develop the discipline of long-term thinking.

3. Reframe your view of business ownership:

When you buy stocks, remind yourself that you're becoming a part-owner of real businesses. Try to think like an owner, not just a trader.

4. Visualize your success:

Create a vision board or write a detailed description of what your life will look like when you've achieved success as a Minimalistic Entrepreneur. Refer to this regularly to stay motivated.

5. Find a community:

Surround yourself with like-minded individuals who share the Minimalistic Entrepreneur mindset. This could be through online forums, local investment clubs, or by following thought leaders in this space.

Remember, becoming a Minimalistic Entrepreneur is as much about mindset as it is about practical skills. By cultivating the right mentality, you'll be well-prepared for the journey ahead.

Key Skills and Knowledge Required

While the right mindset forms the foundation of your journey as a Minimalistic Entrepreneur, it's equally important to develop a specific set of skills and knowledge. These tools will empower you to make informed decisions, manage your portfolio effectively, and navigate the complex world of investing with confidence.

1. Financial Literacy

At the core of Minimalistic Entrepreneurship is a solid understanding of financial concepts. You don't need to be a certified accountant, but a good grasp of the following areas is crucial:
- Basic Accounting: Understanding concepts like assets, liabilities, equity, income, and expenses will help you read and interpret financial statements.
- Time Value of Money: This concept underpins much of finance and investing. It's about understanding that a dollar today is worth more than a dollar in the future due to its earning potential.
- Compound Interest: Often called the "eighth wonder of the world" by Albert Einstein, compound interest is a powerful force in wealth building. Understanding how it works is key to appreciating the long-term potential of your investments.
- Risk and Return: Every investment carries some level of risk. Understanding the relationship between risk and potential returns is crucial for making informed investment decisions.
Practical Step: Start with a basic financial literacy course. Many universities offer free online courses, or you could pick up a beginner's book on personal finance. Websites like Investopedia also offer excellent resources for learning financial terms and concepts.

2. Market Analysis

As a Minimalistic Entrepreneur, the stock market is your arena. Developing strong analytical skills will help you navigate this complex environment:

- Fundamental Analysis: This involves evaluating a company's financial health, competitive position, and growth prospects. Key skills include reading financial statements, understanding business models, and analyzing industry trends.

- Technical Analysis: While not all investors use technical analysis, understanding basics like trends, support and resistance levels, and common chart patterns can be valuable.

- Economic Analysis: The broader economic environment significantly impacts stock performance. Familiarize yourself with key economic indicators like GDP growth, inflation rates, and employment figures.

Practical Step: Choose a company you're interested in and practice doing a fundamental analysis. Look at its recent annual reports, analyze its financial ratios, and research its competitive position. Over time, expand this to comparing companies within the same industry.

3. Investment Strategy Development

Successful Minimalistic Entrepreneurs don't just pick stocks randomly. They develop and refine investment strategies:

- Asset Allocation: Understanding how to divide your investments among different asset classes (like stocks, bonds, and real estate) based on your goals and risk tolerance.

- Diversification: Learning how to spread risk by investing in a variety of sectors and companies.

- Value Investing: Popularized by Benjamin Graham and Warren Buffett, this strategy involves identifying undervalued stocks.

- Growth Investing: This approach focuses on companies with strong growth prospects, even if their current valuations seem high.

- Dividend Investing: A strategy that focuses on stocks that pay regular dividends, providing a steady income stream.

Practical Step: Research different investment strategies and identify one that resonates with your goals and risk tolerance. Create a mock portfolio using this strategy and track its performance over time.

4. Risk Management

Managing risk is crucial for long-term success as a Minimalistic Entrepreneur:

- Portfolio Diversification: Understanding how to spread risk across different investments.

- Position Sizing: Knowing how much of your portfolio to allocate to each investment.

- Stop-Loss Strategies: While long-term holding is generally preferred, knowing when and how to cut losses can be important.

- Hedging: Advanced techniques for protecting your portfolio against market downturns.

Practical Step: Analyze your current or mock portfolio. Are you overly exposed to any single stock or sector? Practice rebalancing your portfolio to manage risk.

5. Emotional Intelligence

Investing can be an emotional rollercoaster. Developing emotional intelligence is crucial:

- Patience: The ability to stick to your strategy even when short-term results are disappointing.

- Discipline: Following your investment rules and not giving in to impulsive decisions.

- Stress Management: Learning to stay calm during market volatility.

- Self-awareness: Understanding your own biases and how they might affect your investment decisions.

Practical Step: Keep an investment journal. Record not just your decisions, but also your emotions and thought processes. Review this regularly to identify patterns and areas for improvement.

6. Technology Skills

In today's digital age, being comfortable with technology is important:

- Using Trading Platforms: Familiarize yourself with online brokerage platforms.

- Financial Software: Learn to use spreadsheet software for financial modeling and portfolio tracking.

- Information Gathering: Develop skills in using the internet effectively for research and staying updated on market news.

Practical Step: If you haven't already, open an account with an online broker. Spend time exploring their platform and tools. Set up a spreadsheet to track your investments and practice updating it regularly.

7. Legal and Tax Knowledge

While you don't need to be a lawyer or tax expert, basic knowledge in these areas is valuable:

- Investment Taxation: Understanding how different investments are taxed can help you make more tax-efficient decisions.

- Retirement Accounts: Knowing the rules and benefits of various retirement accounts like 401(k)s and IRAs.

- Legal Structures: Understanding the basics of different legal structures for your investment activities (e.g., individual, LLC, S-Corp).

Practical Step: Research the tax implications of different types of investment income (e.g., dividends vs. capital gains). If you're in the US, familiarize yourself with the basics of IRA and 401(k) accounts.

Continuous Skill Development

Remember, developing these skills is an ongoing process. The world of finance and investing is always evolving, and successful Minimalistic Entrepreneurs commit to lifelong learning.

Here are some ways to continually develop your skills:

1. Read Widely: Beyond just financial books, read about history, psychology, and technology. A broad knowledge base can give you unique insights.

2. Follow Thought Leaders: Follow successful investors and financial experts on social media or through their writings.

3. Attend Workshops and Seminars: Look for investment workshops or seminars in your area or online.

4. Join Investment Clubs: Connecting with other investors can be a great way to learn and share ideas.

5. Practice with Paper Trading: Many platforms offer paper trading accounts where you can practice your strategies without risking real money.

Setting Your Financial Goals

As a Minimalistic Entrepreneur, having a clear vision of what you want to achieve is crucial. Your financial goals will serve as your North Star, guiding your investment decisions and helping you stay motivated through the ups and downs of your journey. In this section, we'll explore the importance of goal setting and provide a framework for establishing clear, achievable financial objectives.

The Power of Goal Setting

Before we dive into the specifics of how to set financial goals, let's take a moment to appreciate why this step is so crucial:

1. Direction: Goals give you a clear direction, helping you focus your efforts and resources where they matter most.

2. Motivation: Well-defined goals can serve as powerful motivators, especially during challenging times.

3. Measurement: Goals provide benchmarks against which you can measure your progress.

4. Decision-making: Clear goals can help you make better investment decisions by providing a framework for evaluating opportunities.

5. Alignment: Goals ensure that your actions as a Minimalistic Entrepreneur align with your broader life objectives.

The SMART Framework for Goal Setting

When setting your financial goals, it's helpful to use the SMART framework. SMART is an acronym that stands for Specific, Measurable, Achievable, Relevant, and Time-bound. Let's break this down:

1. Specific:

Your goals should be clear and specific, not vague. Instead of "I want to be rich," try "I want to achieve a net worth of $1 million."

2. Measurable:

You should be able to track your progress. "I want to increase my passive income" is not as effective as "I want to generate $3,000 per month in dividend income."

3. Achievable:

While it's good to aim high, your goals should be realistically attainable given your current situation and resources.

4. Relevant:

Your goals should align with your broader life objectives and values.

5. Time-bound:

Set a target date for achieving your goal. This creates a sense of urgency and helps you stay on track.

Types of Financial Goals for Minimalistic Entrepreneurs

As a Minimalistic Entrepreneur, your financial goals might fall into several categories:

1. Net Worth Goals: These relate to your overall financial position. For example, "Achieve a net worth of $500,000 by age 40."

2. Passive Income Goals: These focus on generating income from your investments. For instance, "Generate $5,000 per month in passive income within 10 years."

3. Portfolio Growth Goals: These relate to the growth of your investment portfolio. For example, "Achieve an average annual portfolio growth of 8% over the next 20 years."

4. Diversification Goals: These aim to spread your risk across different types of investments. For instance, "Have no more than 5% of my portfolio in any single stock by the end of next year."

5. Lifestyle Goals: These relate to how your investments will support your desired lifestyle. For example, "Build an investment portfolio that allows me to retire at age 55."

Setting Your Goals: A Step-by-Step Approach

Now that we understand the importance of goal setting and the types of goals you might set, let's walk through a process for establishing your financial goals as a Minimalistic Entrepreneur:

1. Reflect on Your Values and Life Objectives:
Begin by thinking about what truly matters to you. Do you value financial security? Early retirement? The ability to travel extensively? Your financial goals should support your broader life objectives.

2. Assess Your Current Financial Situation:

Take stock of where you are right now. What's your current net worth? How much are you able to invest each month? Understanding your starting point is crucial for setting realistic goals.

3. Envision Your Ideal Future:

Imagine your ideal life 5, 10, or 20 years from now. What does financial success look like to you? This vision will help inform your long-term goals.

4. Set Long-Term Goals:

Based on your vision, set some long-term goals (5-20 years). These might include your ultimate net worth target or the passive income level you hope to achieve for retirement.

5. Establish Medium-Term Goals:

Work backwards from your long-term goals to set medium-term objectives (1-5 years). These serve as milestones on the way to your long-term vision.

6. Define Short-Term Goals:

Finally, set short-term goals (less than 1 year) that will start you on the path toward your medium and long-term objectives. These might include learning goals, saving targets, or initial investment milestones.

7. Make Your Goals SMART:

Review each of your goals to ensure they meet the SMART criteria we discussed earlier.

8. Write Them Down:

The act of writing down your goals makes them more concrete and increases your commitment to achieving them.

9. Share Your Goals:
Consider sharing your goals with a trusted friend, family member, or mentor. This accountability can help keep you on track.

10. Review and Adjust Regularly:
Set a schedule to review your goals regularly (e.g., quarterly or annually). As your circumstances change and you make progress, you may need to adjust your goals.

Example: Sarah's Goal-Setting Journey

Let's look at how this process might work in practice. Meet Sarah, a 30-year-old marketing professional who's just beginning her journey as a Minimalistic Entrepreneur.

After reflecting on her values and assessing her current financial situation, Sarah sets the following goals:

Long-term Goal (20 years):
- "Achieve a net worth of $2 million and generate $8,000 per month in passive income by age 50, allowing me to retire early and travel extensively."

Medium-term Goals (5 years):
- "Build an investment portfolio worth $250,000 by age 35."
- "Generate $1,000 per month in dividend income within 5 years."

Short-term Goals (1 year):
- "Save and invest $1,000 per month consistently for the next 12 months."
- "Complete two online courses on stock market investing within 6 months."
- "Research and invest in my first dividend-paying stock within 3 months."

Sarah writes down these goals, shares them with her partner for accountability, and sets a reminder to review her progress quarterly.

The Role of Flexibility

While setting clear goals is crucial, it's equally important to remain flexible. Life circumstances change, market conditions fluctuate, and new opportunities arise. Your goals should serve as a guide, not a straitjacket.

Be prepared to adjust your goals as needed, but do so thoughtfully and intentionally. If you find yourself constantly changing your goals, it might be a sign that they weren't realistic to begin with, or that you need to reassess your broader life objectives.

Remember, the journey of a Minimalistic Entrepreneur is a marathon, not a sprint. Your goals should challenge you, but also be sustainable over the long term.

CHAPTER THREE

FUNDAMENTALS OF STOCK MARKET INVESTING

In this chapter, we'll dive into the fundamentals of the stock market, starting with an in-depth exploration of how the stock market works, specifically in the Indian context. Whether you are new to investing or have some experience, understanding the stock market's mechanics is crucial for making informed decisions that align with your goals as a Minimalistic Entrepreneur.

The Role of the Stock Market in the Economy

The stock market is often described as the backbone of a country's economy, and this is particularly true in India, where the stock market serves as a critical platform for raising capital, driving economic growth, and creating wealth for investors. At its core, the stock market is a marketplace where shares of publicly traded companies are bought and sold. These transactions allow companies to raise funds for expansion and innovation while providing investors with opportunities to share in the profits and growth of these companies.

For the Indian economy, the stock market is more than just a trading platform; it reflects the economic pulse of the nation. The performance of the stock market is closely watched by policymakers, economists, and the general public as it offers insights into the overall economic health, business confidence, and future growth prospects.

Primary vs. Secondary Markets

The stock market is divided into two main segments: the primary market and the secondary market. Understanding the distinction between these two is essential for anyone looking to invest in stocks.

1. Primary Market:

The primary market is where companies first issue new shares to the public through an Initial Public Offering (IPO). This process allows companies to raise capital directly from investors. For instance, when a company like Zomato or Paytm decides to go public, it offers its shares to the public for the first time in the primary market. Investors purchase these shares at a predetermined price set by the company and its underwriters. The funds raised through this process are used by the company for various purposes such as expanding operations, paying off debt, or funding new projects.

In India, the Securities and Exchange Board of India (SEBI) regulates the primary market to ensure transparency, protect investors, and maintain the integrity of the financial system. SEBI's regulations are designed to prevent fraudulent practices and ensure that companies provide all necessary information to investors before going public.

2. Secondary Market:

Once the shares are issued in the primary market, they become available for trading in the secondary market. This is where most stock market activity occurs. The secondary market is where investors buy and sell shares among themselves at market prices, which fluctuate based on supply and demand dynamics.

The Bombay Stock Exchange (BSE) and the National Stock Exchange (NSE) are the two major stock exchanges in India, where most of this trading occurs. For instance, if you wanted to buy shares of Reliance Industries, you would do so in the secondary market by purchasing them from another investor who is selling, rather than directly from the company. The prices in the secondary market are influenced by a variety of factors, including the company's performance, economic conditions, and market sentiment.

Bull and Bear Markets

The terms "bull market" and "bear market" are frequently used to describe the overall trend of the stock market. Understanding these concepts is crucial as they represent the broader market conditions that can significantly impact your investment strategy.

1. Bull Market:

A bull market is characterized by rising stock prices, often accompanied by strong economic indicators like increasing GDP, low unemployment, and rising corporate profits. In a bull market, investor confidence is high, and there is a general expectation that prices will continue to rise. During such periods, there is often a surge in stock market activity as more investors are willing to buy stocks, driving prices even higher.

Historically, India has experienced several bull markets, such as the one from 2003 to 2008, where the Sensex and Nifty indices saw substantial growth, driven by economic reforms, globalization, and increased foreign investment. For a Minimalistic Entrepreneur, a bull market presents opportunities to build wealth as the value of your investments may grow significantly during these periods.

2. Bear Market:

In contrast, a bear market is marked by falling stock prices and generally occurs when the economy is slowing down or entering a recession. During a bear market, investor confidence wanes, and there is widespread pessimism about future market performance. As a result, investors tend to sell off stocks, leading to further declines in prices.

An example of a bear market in India is the period following the global financial crisis of 2008, when the Sensex and Nifty experienced sharp declines. For Minimalistic Entrepreneurs, bear markets are challenging but also present opportunities. While the value of your investments may decrease, bear markets can offer chances to buy quality stocks at lower prices, setting the stage for future gains when the market recovers.

Understanding Market Indices

Market indices are statistical measures that track the performance of a group of stocks representing a particular segment of the market. In India, the two most prominent indices are the Sensex and the Nifty.

1. Sensex:

The Sensex, or the BSE Sensex, is the benchmark index of the Bombay Stock Exchange (BSE). It comprises 30 of the largest and most actively traded companies on the BSE, representing various sectors of the Indian economy. The Sensex is often used as a barometer for the overall health of the Indian stock market and economy. Companies like Tata Consultancy Services (TCS), Reliance Industries, and HDFC Bank are part of this index. The performance of the Sensex is closely monitored by investors, policymakers, and the media.

2. Nifty:

The Nifty 50, or simply the Nifty, is the benchmark index of the National Stock Exchange (NSE). It consists of 50 of the largest and most liquid stocks on the NSE. Like the Sensex, the Nifty is a key indicator of the market's performance and is widely followed by investors. The Nifty includes companies across different sectors, such as IT, banking, pharmaceuticals, and consumer goods, making it a comprehensive reflection of the Indian economy.

Both the Sensex and Nifty are calculated based on the free-float market capitalization of their constituent stocks, meaning that the index values are determined by the market prices of the companies' shares, adjusted for the proportion of shares available for trading.

Understanding these indices is crucial for Minimalistic Entrepreneurs as they provide a snapshot of market trends and help investors gauge the overall market sentiment. Moreover, these indices serve as benchmarks against which the performance of individual stocks or portfolios can be compared.

The Role of SEBI in Regulating the Indian Stock Market

The Securities and Exchange Board of India (SEBI) plays a vital role in ensuring the smooth functioning of the Indian stock market. Established in 1988 and given statutory powers in 1992, SEBI's primary responsibility is to protect the interests of investors, promote the development of the securities market, and regulate its functioning to ensure fair and transparent dealings.

For Minimalistic Entrepreneurs, understanding SEBI's role is essential as it provides the regulatory framework within which all market participants operate. SEBI oversees everything from the initial public offerings (IPOs) and mutual funds to insider trading and stockbrokers. It enforces rules and regulations designed to prevent fraud, maintain market integrity, and protect retail investors.

One of SEBI's key functions is to ensure that companies provide full and accurate information to the public when issuing shares or other securities. This transparency is crucial for investors to make informed decisions. SEBI also monitors market activities to prevent manipulative practices such as insider trading, where individuals with non-public information about a company use that knowledge to gain an unfair advantage in the market.

The Impact of Foreign Institutional Investors (FIIs) and Domestic Institutional Investors (DIIs)

Foreign Institutional Investors (FIIs) and Domestic Institutional Investors (DIIs) are significant players in the Indian stock market, and their actions can have a profound impact on market dynamics.

1. Foreign Institutional Investors (FIIs):

FIIs refer to investment funds or companies that are based outside of India but invest in Indian financial markets. These include hedge funds, pension funds, and mutual funds. FIIs play a critical role in the Indian stock market, often driving large volumes of trading activity. Their investment decisions are influenced by global economic conditions, currency fluctuations, and geopolitical factors.

When FIIs pour money into the Indian stock market, it often leads to a rise in stock prices and a positive market sentiment. Conversely, when FIIs withdraw funds, it can lead to market corrections or even sharp declines. For Minimalistic Entrepreneurs, keeping an eye on FII activity can provide valuable insights into broader market trends.

2. Domestic Institutional Investors (DIIs):

DIIs are investment entities based within India, such as mutual funds, insurance companies, and pension funds. DIIs also play a crucial role in the stock market, especially in balancing the influence of FIIs. During periods of FII outflows, DIIs often step in to buy stocks, providing stability to the market.

The presence of strong DIIs is essential for the Indian stock market as it ensures that domestic savings are channeled into productive investments within the country. For Minimalistic Entrepreneurs, understanding the role of DIIs can help in anticipating market movements and making informed investment decisions.

Market Sentiment and Investor Behavior

Market sentiment refers to the overall attitude of investors toward the stock market. It is often driven by factors such as economic news, political events, corporate earnings reports, and global market trends. Market sentiment can be bullish (optimistic) or bearish (pessimistic), and it plays a crucial role in determining stock prices.

In India, investor behavior is influenced by a unique mix of factors, including cultural attitudes toward money, the historical performance of markets, and the influence of financial media. For instance, during the bull market from 2003 to 2008,

Types of Stocks and Investment Vehicles

In this Part, we'll take a deep dive into the various types of stocks and investment vehicles available in the Indian market. Understanding these options is crucial for any Minimalistic Entrepreneur looking to build a portfolio that aligns with their financial goals, risk tolerance, and long-term vision. This chapter is not just about knowing what's out there, but about empowering you to make informed decisions that will help you achieve financial freedom.

The Power of Ownership: Common Stocks vs. Preferred Stocks

At the heart of stock market investing lies the concept of ownership. When you buy a share of stock, you're essentially buying a piece of a company. But not all shares are created equal. In the Indian market, the two primary types of stocks you can invest in are common stocks and preferred stocks. Each comes with its own set of advantages and considerations, and understanding these differences will help you make choices that are right for you.

1. Common Stocks: Common stocks are the most prevalent type of stock that investors buy and sell. When you purchase common stock in a company, you become a part-owner of that company. This ownership comes with certain rights, such as voting on important company matters and, most importantly, the potential to earn dividends and capital gains.

In India, companies like Reliance Industries, Infosys, and HDFC Bank issue common stocks. These stocks are what most investors think of when they talk about "the stock market." The value of common stocks can fluctuate based on the company's performance, market conditions, and investor sentiment. One of the most appealing aspects of common stocks is their potential for capital appreciation. As the company grows and becomes more profitable, the value of its shares can increase, leading to substantial gains for investors.

However, with the potential for high returns comes higher risk. Common stocks are subject to market volatility, and their prices can swing dramatically in response to economic news, company performance, or broader market trends. For Minimalistic Entrepreneurs, investing in common stocks requires a willingness to ride out these fluctuations and a belief in the long-term growth of the companies in which you invest.

2. Preferred Stocks: Preferred stocks are less common than their "common" counterparts but offer unique benefits that might appeal to certain investors. In the Indian context, preferred stocks function as a hybrid between common stocks and bonds. They provide a fixed dividend, which is paid out before any dividends are given to common stockholders, and they typically have less price volatility than common stocks.

The primary advantage of preferred stocks is the fixed income they provide. This makes them attractive to investors seeking regular income, such as retirees or those looking to balance a more volatile portfolio. However, preferred stocks generally do not offer the same potential for capital appreciation as common stocks. Additionally, preferred shareholders typically do not have voting rights, meaning they have less influence over company decisions.

For the Minimalistic Entrepreneur, preferred stocks can serve as a more stable income source within a diversified portfolio. They can help reduce overall portfolio risk while still providing a steady stream of dividends. However, it's important to remember that while preferred stocks may be safer, they often come with lower returns than common stocks over the long term.

Growth Stocks vs. Value Stocks: Finding Your Investment Style

As you navigate the Indian stock market, you'll encounter different types of stocks categorized by their growth potential and current market value. Understanding whether a stock is classified as a growth stock or a value stock can help you align your investments with your financial goals and risk tolerance.

1. Growth Stocks: Growth stocks represent companies that are expected to grow at an above-average rate compared to other companies in the market. These are often companies in industries like technology, pharmaceuticals, or renewable energy, where innovation and expansion drive significant revenue growth.

In India, companies like Infosys, TCS, and Bajaj Finance are often considered growth stocks. These companies reinvest their earnings into expanding operations, developing new products, or entering new markets, rather than paying out large dividends. As a result, growth stocks tend to have higher price-to-earnings (P/E) ratios and can offer substantial returns if the company's growth projections are met or exceeded.

However, investing in growth stocks also comes with higher risk. These stocks are often more volatile because their prices are based on future expectations rather than current performance. If a company fails to meet growth expectations, its stock price can decline sharply. For the Minimalistic Entrepreneur, growth stocks are ideal if you're willing to take on more risk in exchange for the possibility of higher returns. They are particularly suited to younger investors or those with a longer investment horizon who can afford to ride out periods of volatility.

2. Value Stocks: Value stocks, on the other hand, represent companies that are currently undervalued by the market. These companies may have solid fundamentals, such as steady earnings, strong balance sheets, and established market positions, but their stock prices may be lower than what their financial performance would suggest. This could be due to temporary setbacks, market downturns, or simply being overlooked by investors.

Examples of value stocks in India include companies like ITC, Coal India, and NTPC, which have stable earnings and often pay higher-than-average dividends. Value investing is based on the principle of buying low and selling high. By purchasing stocks that are undervalued, you can potentially profit as the market corrects itself and these stocks return to their intrinsic value.

Value stocks are generally less volatile than growth stocks and can provide a margin of safety, making them attractive to more conservative investors or those seeking steady returns. For the Minimalistic Entrepreneur, value stocks offer a way to build wealth with lower risk. They are particularly beneficial in a diversified portfolio, where they can provide stability and income, balancing out the more speculative nature of growth stocks.

Mutual Funds and Exchange-Traded Funds (ETFs): Diversification Made Easy

For many investors, the idea of picking individual stocks can be daunting. This is where mutual funds and exchange-traded funds (ETFs) come into play. These investment vehicles allow you to invest in a diversified portfolio of stocks with a single purchase, providing instant diversification and professional management.

1. Mutual Funds: Mutual funds are one of the most popular investment vehicles in India, especially for those new to investing. A mutual fund pools money from multiple investors to invest in a diversified portfolio of stocks, bonds, or other securities. Each mutual fund is managed by a professional fund manager, who makes decisions about which securities to buy and sell based on the fund's investment objectives.

In India, mutual funds come in various types, including equity funds, debt funds, balanced funds, and index funds. For instance, an equity mutual fund might invest primarily in stocks, while a debt mutual fund would focus on bonds. The biggest advantage of mutual funds is that they provide diversification and professional management, reducing the risk associated with investing in individual stocks.

Mutual funds in India are regulated by SEBI, ensuring transparency and protection for investors. They are ideal for Minimalistic Entrepreneurs who prefer a hands-off approach to investing or those who want to diversify their portfolios without having to pick individual stocks. However, it's important to be aware of the fees associated with mutual funds, which can eat into your returns over time.

2. Exchange-Traded Funds (ETFs): ETFs are similar to mutual funds in that they offer diversification by investing in a basket of securities. However, unlike mutual funds, which are priced once at the end of each trading day, ETFs trade on stock exchanges throughout the day, just like individual stocks. This means you can buy and sell ETFs at market prices, giving you more flexibility.

In India, ETFs have gained popularity due to their lower expense ratios compared to mutual funds and their ability to provide exposure to specific sectors or indices. For example, the Nifty 50 ETF allows you to invest in the 50 largest companies on the NSE, mirroring the performance of the Nifty index.

ETFs are an excellent choice for Minimalistic Entrepreneurs looking for a cost-effective way to diversify their portfolios. They offer the best of both worlds: the diversification of a mutual fund with the flexibility of a stock. ETFs are also ideal for implementing specific investment strategies, such as focusing on particular sectors like technology or energy, or tracking a broad market index.

Sectoral and Thematic Investing: Targeting Specific Opportunities

Sectoral and thematic investing are strategies that allow you to focus on specific areas of the market that you believe will outperform over time. This approach can be particularly appealing for Minimalistic Entrepreneurs who want to align their investments with their personal interests or beliefs.

1. Sectoral Investing: Sectoral investing involves investing in specific sectors of the economy, such as technology, healthcare, or energy. This strategy is based on the belief that certain sectors will perform better than others due to economic trends, technological advancements, or changes in consumer behavior.

In India, sectoral mutual funds and ETFs are available for various sectors, allowing you to focus your investments on areas you believe have strong growth potential. For example, a technology sector fund might invest in companies like Infosys, Wipro, and HCL Technologies, which are leaders in the IT industry. Sectoral investing can be rewarding but also comes with higher risk, as your returns will be heavily dependent on the performance of that particular sector.

2. Thematic Investing: Thematic investing takes sectoral investing a step further by focusing on broader themes that cut across multiple sectors. Themes could include renewable energy, digital transformation, or urbanization. Thematic investing is about identifying long-term trends that will drive growth and investing in companies that stand to benefit from these trends.

For example, in India, thematic funds might focus on renewable energy, investing in companies involved in solar power, wind energy, and electric vehicles. Another theme could be digital India, with investments in technology companies, e-commerce, and digital payments.

Thematic investing allows you to align your investments with your personal beliefs or the trends you are passionate about. It's a way to invest in the future you want to see, whether it's a greener planet, a more connected world, or a tech-driven economy. However, like sectoral investing, thematic investing can be volatile, and it's essential to research and understand the risks associated with each theme.

Real Estate Investment Trusts (REITs): Investing in Real Estate Without Owning Property

For many Indians, real estate is a preferred investment choice. However, directly owning property comes with its own set of challenges, such as high capital requirements, maintenance issues, and liquidity constraints. Real Estate Investment Trusts (REITs) offer an alternative way to invest in real estate without the hassles of property ownership.

1. What are REITs?: REITs are companies that own, operate, or finance income-generating real estate across various sectors, such as commercial properties, malls, office buildings, and hotels. In India, REITs allow you to invest in real estate in a way that's similar to buying stocks. When you invest in a REIT, you are essentially buying a share of a portfolio of properties, and you earn income from the rent collected on those properties.

REITs are traded on stock exchanges, providing liquidity and making it easy to buy and sell shares. They are regulated by SEBI, ensuring transparency and investor protection. For Minimalistic Entrepreneurs, REITs offer a way to diversify into real estate with a relatively small investment and without the need to manage properties directly.

2. Advantages of REITs: The primary advantage of investing in REITs is the ability to earn regular income through dividends, which are often higher than those of common stocks. Additionally, REITs provide exposure to real estate, an asset class that typically has low correlation with stocks and bonds, helping to diversify your portfolio.

Another benefit is the liquidity that REITs offer. Unlike direct real estate investments, where selling a property can take months or even years, REITs can be bought and sold on stock exchanges just like any other stock, providing greater flexibility.

REITs in India, such as Embassy Office Parks REIT and Mindspace Business Parks REIT, have gained popularity among investors looking for stable income and diversification. For the Minimalistic Entrepreneur, REITs are an excellent way to add real estate exposure to your portfolio without the complexities of property management.

In Conclusion, Understanding the various types of stocks and investment vehicles available in the Indian market is the first step in crafting a portfolio that aligns with your goals as a Minimalistic Entrepreneur. Whether you're drawn to the potential high returns of growth stocks, the stability of preferred stocks, the diversification of mutual funds and ETFs, or the income potential of REITs, there's an investment option that fits your needs.

As you move forward, remember that the key to successful investing is diversification. By spreading your investments across different asset classes, sectors, and themes, you can reduce risk and increase your chances of achieving your financial goals. The Indian stock market offers a wealth of opportunities, and with the right knowledge and strategy, you can harness these opportunities to build lasting wealth and achieve financial freedom.

Key Terms and Concepts in Stock Market Investing

Now that we've explored the types of stocks and investment vehicles, it's time to familiarize ourselves with the key terms and concepts that every Minimalistic Entrepreneur must understand to navigate the stock market effectively. Understanding these terms is not just about knowing the definitions but about gaining the confidence to make informed decisions that align with your financial goals.

In this chapter, we'll break down the jargon, demystify the concepts, and show you how to apply this knowledge to your investment strategy. By the end of this chapter, you'll be equipped with the vocabulary and understanding you need to engage with the stock market like a seasoned investor.

Market Capitalization: The Size of the Prize

Market capitalization, often referred to as "market cap," is one of the most fundamental concepts in stock market investing. It represents the total market value of a company's outstanding shares of stock. In simpler terms, market cap gives you an idea of how large a company is in terms of its market value.

How is Market Cap Calculated?

Market cap is calculated by multiplying the current share price by the total number of outstanding shares. For example, if a company has 10 million shares outstanding, and each share is priced at ₹100, the company's market cap would be ₹1,000 million (₹1 billion).

Categories of Market Cap

In the Indian stock market, companies are typically classified into three categories based on their market cap:

1. Large-Cap Stocks: These are the giants of the stock market, with market caps typically over ₹20,000 crores. Large-cap companies are well-established, often industry leaders, and considered safer investments due to their stability. Examples include Reliance Industries, HDFC Bank,

and Infosys.

2. Mid-Cap Stocks: Mid-cap companies have market caps between ₹ 5,000 crores and ₹20,000 crores. These companies are usually in the growth phase and have the potential to become large-cap companies in the future. While they offer higher growth potential than large-cap stocks, they also come with higher risk. Examples include companies like Jubilant FoodWorks and Voltas.

3. Small-Cap Stocks: Small-cap companies have market caps below ₹ 5,000 crores. These are often younger companies with significant growth potential but also come with higher risk due to their size and market position. Investing in small-cap stocks can be rewarding but requires careful research and a higher risk tolerance. Examples include companies like TTK Prestige and Amara Raja Batteries.

Why is Market Cap Important?

Market cap is important because it helps investors assess the size and risk profile of a company. Generally, large-cap stocks are more stable and less volatile, making them suitable for conservative investors. On the other hand, mid-cap and small-cap stocks offer more growth potential but come with greater risk.

For the Minimalistic Entrepreneur, understanding market cap is crucial for building a diversified portfolio. A well-balanced portfolio might include a mix of large-cap, mid-cap, and small-cap stocks to balance stability with growth potential.

Price-to-Earnings Ratio (P/E Ratio): Gauging Value and Growth

The Price-to-Earnings ratio, or P/E ratio, is one of the most commonly used metrics to evaluate a stock's value. It tells you how much investors are willing to pay for each rupee of a company's earnings. The P/E ratio is calculated by dividing the current market price of a stock by its earnings per share (EPS).

Understanding the P/E Ratio

For example, if a company's stock is trading at ₹200 and its earnings per share (EPS) is ₹20, the P/E ratio would be 10. This means investors are willing to pay ₹10 for every rupee the company earns.

What Does the P/E Ratio Tell You?

1. High P/E Ratio: A high P/E ratio can indicate that a stock is overvalued or that investors expect high growth rates in the future. Growth stocks often have high P/E ratios because investors are willing to pay more for the potential of higher future earnings. However, a high P/E ratio also comes with higher risk if the company fails to meet growth expectations.

2. Low P/E Ratio: A low P/E ratio may suggest that a stock is undervalued or that the market has low expectations for the company's future earnings growth. Value investors often seek out stocks with low P/E ratios, believing that they are buying at a discount. However, a low P/E ratio could also indicate underlying problems with the company that investors are wary of.

Using the P/E Ratio in Your Investment Strategy

The P/E ratio is a useful tool for comparing the valuation of companies within the same industry. It's important to compare apples to apples—comparing the P/E ratios of companies in different industries may not provide meaningful insights due to varying industry norms.

For the Minimalistic Entrepreneur, the P/E ratio can be a valuable indicator when selecting stocks. However, it should not be used in isolation. It's essential to consider other factors, such as the company's growth prospects, industry trends, and overall market conditions, when making investment decisions.

Dividends and Yield: Earning While You Hold

Dividends are payments made by a company to its shareholders, usually in the form of cash or additional shares. Dividends represent a portion of the company's profits distributed to shareholders as a reward for their investment.

How Do Dividends Work?

Not all companies pay dividends, but those that do typically distribute them on a regular basis—quarterly, semi-annually, or annually. Dividends provide investors with a source of income in addition to any capital gains they may earn from the increase in the stock's price.

For example, if you own 100 shares of a company that pays an annual dividend of ₹10 per share, you would receive ₹1,000 in dividends each year.

Understanding Dividend Yield

Dividend yield is a financial ratio that shows how much a company pays out in dividends each year relative to its share price. It is calculated by dividing the annual dividend per share by the current share price and multiplying by 100 to express it as a percentage.

For example, if a company's share price is ₹200 and it pays an annual dividend of ₹10, the dividend yield would be 5% (₹10 / ₹200 100).

Why Are Dividends Important?

Dividends are an important consideration for investors looking for steady income from their investments. They are particularly attractive during periods of market volatility when stock prices may not appreciate significantly. For the Minimalistic Entrepreneur, dividends can provide a reliable income stream, which can be reinvested to purchase more shares and benefit from the power of compounding.

However, it's important to remember that not all companies pay dividends. Growth companies, for example, may choose to reinvest profits back into the business rather than paying dividends to shareholders. Therefore, when selecting dividend-paying stocks, it's essential to consider the company's overall financial health and its ability to maintain or increase dividend payments over time.

Volatility and Beta: Understanding Risk

Volatility is a measure of how much the price of a stock fluctuates over time. It's an indicator of the level of risk associated with a particular stock or market. High volatility means the stock's price can change dramatically in a short period, while low volatility indicates more stable price movements.

What is Beta?

Beta is a metric that measures a stock's volatility relative to the overall market. The market has a beta of 1.0. If a stock has a beta greater than 1.0, it's considered more volatile than the market, meaning it's likely to experience larger price swings. A beta less than 1.0 indicates that the stock is less volatile than the market.

For example, a stock with a beta of 1.2 is 20% more volatile than the market. This means that if the market rises by 10%, the stock might rise by 12%, and if the market falls by 10%, the stock might fall by 12%.

Why is Beta Important?

Beta is important because it helps investors understand the risk they're taking on with a particular stock. A higher beta means higher risk, but also the potential for higher returns. Conversely, a lower beta suggests lower risk but also potentially lower returns.

For the Minimalistic Entrepreneur, understanding beta is crucial for managing risk in your portfolio. If you're risk-averse or nearing retirement, you may want to focus on stocks with lower beta values to reduce volatility. On the other hand, if you're young and have a long investment horizon, you might be willing to take on higher beta stocks for the potential of greater returns.

Earnings Per Share (EPS): Measuring Profitability

Earnings per share (EPS) is a key financial metric that indicates how much profit a company generates for each outstanding share of stock. It is calculated by dividing the company's net income by the number of outstanding shares.

Why is EPS Important?

EPS is a direct measure of a company's profitability and is often used by investors to gauge a company's financial health. A higher EPS indicates that the company is generating more profit per share, which can be a sign of strong financial performance.

For example, if a company has a net income of ₹100 crores and 10 crore shares outstanding, its EPS would be ₹10.

Using EPS in Investment Decisions

EPS is a critical factor in determining a company's P/E ratio and assessing its overall value. It's also a key metric for growth investors, as increasing EPS over time can indicate a company's potential for growth.

For the Minimalistic Entrepreneur, tracking EPS can help you identify companies with strong profit growth potential. However, it's important to look at EPS in conjunction with other metrics, such as revenue growth, profit margins, and return on equity, to get a complete picture of a company's financial health.

Return on Equity (ROE): Evaluating Efficiency

Return on Equity (ROE) is a financial ratio that measures a company's ability to generate profits from its shareholders' equity. It's calculated by dividing net income by shareholders' equity and is expressed as a percentage.

Why is ROE Important?

ROE indicates how efficiently a company is using its equity to generate profits. A higher ROE suggests that the company is more effective at converting the money invested by shareholders into profit.

For example, if a company has a net income of ₹50 crores and shareholders' equity of ₹250 crores, its ROE would be 20% (₹50 crores / ₹250 crores 100).

Using ROE in Your Investment Strategy

ROE is a valuable tool for comparing the profitability of companies in the same industry. It's particularly useful for assessing the efficiency of management in generating returns for shareholders.

For the Minimalistic Entrepreneur, a high ROE can be an indicator of a well-managed company with strong growth potential. However, it's important to consider ROE alongside other financial metrics and to understand the factors driving it. For example, a high ROE can sometimes result from high debt levels, which might indicate higher risk.

Debt-to-Equity Ratio: Assessing Financial Leverage

The Debt-to-Equity (D/E) ratio is a measure of a company's financial leverage, calculated by dividing its total liabilities by shareholders' equity. This ratio indicates the proportion of debt a company is using to finance its assets relative to the equity invested by shareholders.

Why is the D/E Ratio Important?

The D/E ratio is important because it helps investors understand the level of financial risk a company is taking on. A higher D/E ratio suggests that the company relies more on debt to finance its operations, which can increase financial risk, especially if the company faces difficulties in meeting its debt obligations.

For example, if a company has total liabilities of ₹200 crores and shareholders' equity of ₹100 crores, its D/E ratio would be 2.0. This means the company has twice as much debt as equity.

Using the D/E Ratio in Investment Decisions

The D/E ratio is particularly useful for assessing the risk associated with investing in a company. For the Minimalistic Entrepreneur, a lower D/E ratio might indicate a safer investment, as the company is less reliant on debt. However, some industries, such as utilities, typically operate with higher D/E ratios due to the nature of their capital-intensive businesses.

When using the D/E ratio in your investment strategy, it's essential to compare companies within the same industry, as acceptable levels of debt can vary significantly between sectors.

In conclusion, Understanding these key terms and concepts is like having a toolkit that you can rely on as you navigate the stock market. Each term offers valuable insights that can help you make more informed and confident investment decisions.

As a Minimalistic Entrepreneur, your goal is to build a portfolio that aligns with your financial goals while managing risk effectively. By mastering these concepts, you are well on your way to becoming a knowledgeable and empowered investor, ready to take control of your financial future.

Remember, investing is a journey, not a destination. Continuously educating yourself and staying informed about market trends will ensure that you remain on the path to financial independence and success. Keep this knowledge at the forefront of your investment decisions, and you'll be well-equipped to achieve the long-term wealth and financial freedom you seek.

CHAPTER FOUR

GETTING STARTED IN THE STOCK MARKET

Opening a Brokerage Account

Now that you've armed yourself with the fundamental concepts of the stock market, it's time to take the first actionable step towards your journey as a Minimalistic Entrepreneur: opening a brokerage account. This might sound like a mundane task, but choosing the right brokerage account is one of the most crucial decisions you'll make. It's the gateway to the stock market and will serve as your primary tool for managing your investments. In this chapter, we'll walk you through the process of selecting and opening a brokerage account in India, tailored to your needs and financial goals.

Why You Need a Brokerage Account

A brokerage account is essentially your personal portal to the stock market. It's through this account that you will buy and sell stocks, mutual funds, ETFs, bonds, and other investment vehicles. Without a brokerage account, you can't directly participate in the stock market.

But it's more than just a tool for trading. The right brokerage account can provide you with the resources, tools, and support you need to succeed as an investor. It can offer insights, research reports, educational materials, and customer support to guide you on your investment journey. Think of it as your financial command center—a place where you can track your investments, analyze your portfolio, and make decisions that will shape your financial future.

Choosing the Right Brokerage Firm

In India, there are numerous brokerage firms, each offering different features, pricing structures, and levels of service. Choosing the right one depends on your investment style, goals, and the kind of support you need as you embark on this journey.

Here's a step-by-step guide to help you make an informed decision:

1. Identify Your Investment Needs and Goals:

Before you start comparing brokerage firms, take a moment to clarify what you're looking for. Are you planning to actively trade stocks, or are you more interested in a long-term investment strategy? Do you need access to extensive research and analysis, or are you comfortable making decisions on your own?

If you're a beginner or prefer a hands-off approach, you might want a brokerage that offers robust customer support, educational resources, and easy-to-use tools. If you're more experienced or plan to trade frequently, you might prioritize low trading fees, advanced trading platforms, and access to detailed market analysis.

2. Understand the Types of Brokerage Firms:

In India, there are two main types of brokerage firms: full-service brokers and discount brokers. Understanding the differences between them will help you choose the one that aligns with your needs.

- Full-Service Brokers: These brokers offer a comprehensive range of services, including financial planning, investment advice, research reports, and portfolio management. They often have dedicated relationship managers who can provide personalized guidance. However, these services come at a higher cost, with full-service brokers typically charging higher brokerage fees and commissions. Examples of full-service brokers in India include ICICI Direct, HDFC Securities, and Kotak Securities.

- Discount Brokers: Discount brokers, on the other hand, offer minimal services but at a much lower cost. They provide the essential platform for buying and selling stocks but do not offer personalized advice or extensive research support. Discount brokers are ideal for self-directed investors who are comfortable managing their portfolios independently. Examples of popular discount brokers in India include Zerodha, Upstox, and 5paisa.

For the Minimalistic Entrepreneur, discount brokers are often a more cost-effective choice, especially if you plan to invest in the long term without frequent trading. However, if you value personalized service and are willing to pay for it, a full-service broker might be more suitable.

3. Compare Brokerage Fees and Commissions:

Brokerage fees and commissions can significantly impact your investment returns, especially if you're not careful. When comparing brokerage firms, it's important to understand their fee structures and how they align with your investment strategy.

- Account Opening Fees: Some brokers charge a one-time fee to open a Demat and trading account. Many discount brokers offer free account opening or charge a nominal fee, while full-service brokers may charge more.

- Brokerage Charges: This is the fee you pay each time you buy or sell a security. Full-service brokers typically charge a percentage of the transaction value, while discount brokers usually charge a flat fee per trade. For long-term investors, these fees can add up, so choosing a broker with low brokerage charges is crucial.

- Annual Maintenance Charges (AMC): Most brokers charge an annual fee for maintaining your Demat account. This fee can vary widely, so be sure to check it before opening an account.

- Other Fees: Brokers may also charge fees for additional services such as fund transfers, statement requests, or access to premium research. Make sure you're aware of all potential fees before making your decision.

For the Minimalistic Entrepreneur, keeping costs low is key to maximizing your investment returns. Discount brokers with flat-fee structures are often the best option, but it's important to ensure they offer the tools and support you need.

4. Evaluate the Trading Platform:

The trading platform is the software or interface you'll use to place trades, monitor your portfolio, and access research and analysis. A user-friendly and reliable platform is essential for managing your investments efficiently.

- Ease of Use: The platform should be intuitive and easy to navigate, especially if you're new to investing. Look for a platform with a clean interface, clear instructions, and simple processes for placing trades and managing your account.

- Tools and Features: Depending on your investment style, you may need access to various tools such as real-time market data, charting tools, technical indicators, and stock screeners. Advanced traders may require more sophisticated tools, while beginners might prefer a simpler platform.

- Mobile App: In today's fast-paced world, having access to your brokerage account on the go is crucial. Check if the broker offers a mobile app that's as functional and user-friendly as the desktop platform.

- Reliability: The platform should be reliable, with minimal downtime, especially during market hours. The last thing you want is to be unable to execute a trade due to technical issues.

For the Minimalistic Entrepreneur, the ideal platform balances ease of use with the necessary tools and features to support your investment strategy. Many discount brokers in India, such as Zerodha with its Kite platform, offer excellent trading platforms that are both affordable and feature-rich.

5. Consider Customer Support and Service:

Even the most seasoned investors need support from time to time. Whether it's technical assistance, account queries, or guidance on specific trades, good customer support can make a significant difference in your investing experience.

- Availability: Check if the broker offers customer support during market hours and whether they provide multiple channels of communication, such as phone, email, and live chat.

- Responsiveness: Quick and efficient service is crucial, especially if you encounter issues during trading hours. Read reviews and testimonials to gauge the broker's reputation for customer service.

- Educational Resources: Some brokers offer extensive educational materials, including webinars, tutorials, and articles, to help you learn and grow as an investor. This can be particularly valuable if you're new to investing or want to deepen your knowledge.

For the Minimalistic Entrepreneur, having reliable customer support can provide peace of mind, especially in the early stages of your investing journey. It's worth considering brokers that offer strong customer service, even if it means paying slightly higher fees.

The Account Opening Process

Once you've chosen the right brokerage firm, the next step is to open your account. In India, this typically involves opening two accounts: a Demat account and a trading account.

1. Demat Account: A Demat account, short for "dematerialized account," is where your shares are stored in electronic form. It's like a digital vault that holds all your securities, eliminating the need for physical share certificates. All trades you execute will be reflected in your Demat account, showing your holdings at any given time.

2. Trading Account: A trading account is linked to your Demat account and is used to place buy and sell orders on the stock market. It acts as the interface between you and the stock exchange, enabling you to execute trades.

Here's a step-by-step guide to opening your brokerage account:

1. Online Application: Most brokers in India allow you to open a brokerage account online. Visit the broker's website or download their mobile app to start the application process. You'll be asked to provide personal details such as your name, address, PAN card number, and contact information.

2. Document Submission: You'll need to upload several documents to complete your application. These typically include:

- PAN Card: A Permanent Account Number (PAN) card is mandatory for opening a brokerage account in India.

- Aadhaar Card: Your Aadhaar card serves as proof of identity and address.

- Bank Statement: A recent bank statement is required to verify your bank account details for fund transfers.

- Photograph: A passport-sized photograph is usually required as part of the application.

3. In-Person Verification (IPV): SEBI regulations require an In-Person Verification (IPV) to verify your identity. This can often be done online via a video call, where you'll be asked to show your PAN card and Aadhaar card.

4. Account Activation: Once your documents are verified, your Demat and trading accounts will be activated, and you'll receive login credentials for the trading platform. This process usually takes a few days, depending on the broker.

5. Linking Your Bank Account: After your account is activated, you'll need to link your bank account to your trading account for seamless fund transfers. This will allow you to deposit funds into your trading account and withdraw profits directly to your bank account.

6. Depositing Funds: To start investing, you'll need to deposit funds into your trading account. Most brokers offer multiple ways to transfer money, including NEFT, RTGS, UPI, and net banking.

Security and Safety Considerations

Security is paramount when dealing with financial accounts, and your brokerage account is no exception. Here are some tips to ensure the safety of your account:

- Strong Passwords: Use a strong, unique password for your brokerage account and change it regularly. Avoid using easily guessable passwords like birthdays or common words.

- Two-Factor Authentication (2FA): Enable two-factor authentication (2FA) for an extra layer of security. This requires you to verify your identity through a second method, such as a one-time password (OTP) sent to your mobile phone.

- Beware of Phishing Scams: Be cautious of phishing emails or messages that ask for your login credentials. Always verify the authenticity of any communication from your broker.

- Monitor Your Account: Regularly review your account statements and transaction history to ensure there are no unauthorized activities.

Opening a brokerage account is the first tangible step in your journey as a Minimalistic Entrepreneur. It's the bridge between your financial goals and the opportunities that the stock market offers. By choosing the right brokerage firm, understanding the fee structures, and ensuring your account is secure, you're setting the foundation for a successful investing experience.

Remember, this is just the beginning. Your brokerage account is not just a place to trade stocks—it's your command center for building wealth and achieving financial freedom. Take the time to choose wisely, set up your account securely, and you'll be well on your way to mastering the stock market as a Minimalistic Entrepreneur.

Researching and Selecting Stocks

With your brokerage account up and running, you're ready to take the next significant step: researching and selecting stocks. This is where the journey becomes both exciting and challenging. The stock market offers countless opportunities, but navigating through them requires a strategic approach, informed decision-making, and a bit of patience.

In this chapter, we'll walk you through the process of researching stocks, understanding key factors to consider, and ultimately selecting the right stocks that align with your financial goals. This isn't just about picking any stock; it's about choosing investments that are well-suited to your strategy as a Minimalistic Entrepreneur, helping you build a portfolio that will stand the test of time.

The Importance of Research: Knowledge is Power

Before you put your hard-earned money into any stock, it's crucial to do your homework. Investing without proper research is like setting sail without a map—you might get lucky, but you're more likely to end up lost at sea. The stock market is filled with opportunities, but not every opportunity is right for you. Researching stocks thoroughly ensures that your investments are based on solid information rather than speculation or emotion.

Research helps you understand a company's financial health, growth potential, and the risks involved in investing in its stock. It also gives you the confidence to make informed decisions and stay committed to your investment strategy, even when the market experiences turbulence.

Where to Begin: Sources of Information

When it comes to researching stocks, the good news is that you have a wealth of information at your fingertips. The challenge is knowing where to look and how to interpret the data you find. Here are some key sources of information that you can use to research stocks effectively:

1. Company Financial Statements: One of the most reliable sources of information about a company is its financial statements. These documents provide a detailed overview of the company's financial performance, including its income, expenses, assets, and liabilities.

- Balance Sheet: The balance sheet shows a company's assets, liabilities, and shareholders' equity at a specific point in time. It's a snapshot of the company's financial health and its ability to meet short-term and long-term obligations.

- Income Statement: The income statement, also known as the profit and loss (P&L) statement, shows the company's revenues, expenses, and profits over a specific period, usually a quarter or a year. It's a key indicator of the company's profitability and operational efficiency.

- Cash Flow Statement: The cash flow statement tracks the flow of cash in and out of the company. It helps you understand how well the company generates cash to meet its debt obligations, pay dividends, and invest in growth.

2. Annual Reports: Annual reports are comprehensive documents that provide detailed information about a company's operations, financial performance, and future outlook. They typically include a letter from the CEO, financial statements, management's discussion and analysis (MD&A), and information about the company's strategy and goals.

Reading annual reports can give you a deeper understanding of the company's business model, competitive advantages, and the challenges it faces. It also allows you to assess the company's management team and their approach to creating shareholder value.

3. Earnings Calls and Transcripts: Companies often hold earnings calls after releasing their quarterly or annual results. During these calls, the management team discusses the company's performance, provides guidance for future quarters, and answers questions from analysts. Earnings call transcripts are also available for those who prefer to read rather than listen.

Participating in or reading the transcripts of earnings calls can provide valuable insights into the company's recent performance, management's perspective on challenges and opportunities, and any changes in the company's strategy.

4. Analyst Reports: Many brokerage firms and financial institutions publish analyst reports that provide in-depth analysis of specific companies, industries, and market trends. These reports often include stock ratings

(e.g., buy, hold, sell), price targets, and detailed analyses of a company's financials, market position, and competitive landscape.

While analyst reports can be helpful, it's important to remember that they are just one piece of the puzzle. Analysts have their own biases and may not always get it right. Use these reports as a starting point, but always conduct your own research.

5. News and Media: Keeping up with financial news is essential for staying informed about market trends, economic developments, and company-specific events that could impact your investments. Websites like Moneycontrol, Economic Times, and BloombergQuint provide up-to-date news, market analysis, and expert opinions.

However, it's important to approach news with a critical eye. The financial media often focuses on short-term events and can sometimes amplify market noise. As a Minimalistic Entrepreneur, your focus should be on long-term trends and fundamentals, rather than reacting to every piece of news.

6. Stock Screeners: Stock screeners are online tools that allow you to filter stocks based on specific criteria, such as market cap, P/E ratio, dividend yield, and more. They are incredibly useful for narrowing down your options and identifying stocks that meet your investment criteria.

Most brokerage platforms in India offer built-in stock screeners, but there are also several standalone tools available online. By inputting your desired parameters, you can generate a list of potential stocks to research further.

Key Factors to Consider When Selecting Stocks

Now that you know where to find information, the next step is to understand what to look for. Selecting the right stocks requires a careful evaluation of various factors that can influence a company's performance and its stock price. Here are some key factors to consider:

1. Company Fundamentals:

The fundamental analysis involves evaluating a company's financial health, profitability, and growth potential. Here's what to focus on:

- Revenue Growth: Look for companies with consistent revenue growth over the past few years. Steady growth indicates a strong business model and increasing demand for the company's products or services.

- Profit Margins: Analyze the company's profit margins (gross, operating, and net) to assess its efficiency in managing costs and generating profits. Higher margins are generally a positive sign, but it's also important to consider industry benchmarks.

- Return on Equity (ROE): ROE measures how effectively a company is using its shareholders' equity to generate profits. A higher ROE indicates better management efficiency and profitability.

- Debt Levels: Evaluate the company's debt-to-equity ratio to understand its financial leverage. Companies with high levels of debt may be riskier, especially in an economic downturn, as they must meet debt obligations regardless of their profitability.

2. Industry and Market Position:

A company's performance is often influenced by the industry it operates in and its position within that industry. Consider the following:

- Industry Growth Prospects: Invest in industries with strong growth prospects, driven by factors such as technological advancements, demographic trends, or regulatory changes. For example, the IT sector in India has seen significant growth due to the global demand for digital transformation services.

- Market Share: Companies with a dominant market share often have competitive advantages, such as brand recognition, economies of scale, or a loyal customer base. These advantages can help them maintain profitability even in challenging market conditions.

- Competition: Assess the level of competition in the industry. Highly competitive industries can be challenging for companies to maintain pricing power and profit margins. Look for companies with a unique value proposition or competitive edge.

3. Management Quality:

The quality of a company's management team plays a crucial role in its long-term success. Evaluate the following aspects:

- Experience and Track Record: Research the background and experience of the company's key executives, including the CEO, CFO, and board members. A strong leadership team with a proven track record of success is a positive indicator.

- Corporate Governance: Good corporate governance practices, including transparency, accountability, and ethical behavior, are essential for building trust with shareholders. Companies with strong governance are more likely to make decisions that align with shareholder interests.

- Strategic Vision: Consider the management team's strategic vision for the company's future. Are they focused on long-term growth, innovation, and creating shareholder value? Or are they primarily driven by short-term gains? Look for companies where management demonstrates a clear and consistent strategy that aligns with your investment goals.

4. Valuation:

Even if a company has strong fundamentals and a competitive position, it's important to consider whether the stock is fairly valued. Paying too much for a stock can limit your potential returns. Here are some valuation metrics to consider:

- Price-to-Earnings (P/E) Ratio: As discussed in the previous chapter, the P/E ratio compares the stock's current price to its earnings per share. Compare the P/E ratio of the stock to industry peers and the broader market to gauge its valuation.

- Price-to-Book (P/B) Ratio: The P/B ratio compares the stock's market price to its book value (assets minus liabilities). A lower P/B ratio may indicate that the stock is undervalued, especially if the company has strong fundamentals.

- Dividend Yield: For dividend-paying stocks, the dividend yield is an important metric to consider. It represents the annual dividend payment as a percentage of the stock's current price. A higher dividend yield may be attractive for income-focused investors, but it's important to ensure that the company can sustain its dividend payments.

- Discounted Cash Flow (DCF) Analysis: For more advanced investors, DCF analysis is a method of valuing a company based on the present value of its expected future cash flows. This approach requires making assumptions about the company's growth rate, discount rate, and future cash flows, but it can provide a more detailed valuation estimate.

5. Risk Factors:

Every investment comes with risks, and it's important to identify and evaluate these risks before investing in a stock. Consider the following:

- Economic and Industry Risks: Assess the broader economic factors that could impact the company's performance, such as interest rates, inflation, and currency fluctuations. Additionally, consider industry-specific risks, such as changes in technology, regulation, or consumer behavior.

- Company-Specific Risks: Analyze the risks unique to the company, such as reliance on a single product or customer, legal challenges, or management turnover. These factors can affect the company's stability and growth potential.

- Market Sentiment: Market sentiment refers to the overall mood or attitude of investors toward a particular stock or the market as a whole. While sentiment can influence short-term stock prices, it's important to focus on the company's fundamentals and long-term prospects rather than getting swayed by market emotions.

Building a Watchlist: Your Investment Radar

Once you've identified potential stocks through your research, it's helpful to create a watchlist. A watchlist is a curated list of stocks that you're considering for your portfolio. It allows you to monitor these stocks over time, track their performance, and wait for the right buying opportunities.

Here's how to build and manage your watchlist:

1. Select Criteria: Define the criteria for adding stocks to your watchlist. This could include factors such as growth potential, valuation, dividend yield, or industry focus. Make sure the criteria align with your investment goals and strategy.

2. Track Performance: Regularly monitor the performance of the stocks on your watchlist. Use tools like stock charts, price alerts, and news feeds to stay informed about any developments that could impact the stock's performance.

3. Review and Update: Periodically review your watchlist to remove stocks that no longer meet your criteria or add new ones that align with

your goals. Your watchlist should be dynamic and reflect your evolving investment strategy.

Taking the Plunge: Deciding When to Buy

After thorough research and careful consideration, you're ready to make your first investment. But when is the right time to buy a stock? Timing the market perfectly is nearly impossible, but there are strategies you can use to make informed decisions:

1. Dollar-Cost Averaging: Dollar-cost averaging (DCA) is a strategy where you invest a fixed amount of money in a stock at regular intervals, regardless of the stock's price. This approach reduces the impact of market volatility and eliminates the need to time the market. Over time, DCA can help you build a position in a stock at an average cost.

2. Wait for a Pullback: If a stock you're interested in is trading at a high price, consider waiting for a market correction or pullback to buy at a lower price. This strategy requires patience, but it can help you avoid overpaying for a stock.

3. Focus on Long-Term Value: Instead of trying to time the market, focus on the long-term value of the stock. If you believe in the company's growth prospects and the stock is reasonably valued, it may be worth buying even if the market is volatile. Remember, as a Minimalistic Entrepreneur, your goal is to build wealth over time, not to make quick profits.

Researching and selecting stocks is both an art and a science. It requires a combination of analytical skills, strategic thinking, and the discipline to stay focused on your long-term goals. By taking the time to research stocks thoroughly, evaluate key factors, and build a diversified portfolio, you're setting yourself up for success as a Minimalistic Entrepreneur.

Remember, the stock market is a journey, not a destination. Continuous learning, staying informed, and adapting your strategy as needed are all part of the process. With the right approach, you can confidently navigate the stock market and make investment decisions that will help you achieve financial freedom and create lasting wealth.

Understanding Stock Valuation Methods

Having set up your brokerage account and begun researching and selecting stocks, the next step in your journey as a Minimalistic Entrepreneur is understanding how to value those stocks. Valuation is the process of determining what a stock is worth, and it's a critical skill for any investor. Whether you're considering a stock for long-term investment or a short-term trade, understanding its intrinsic value can help you make better decisions.

In this chapter, we'll explore different stock valuation methods, from fundamental analysis to technical analysis, and how you can apply these techniques to build a portfolio that aligns with your financial goals. We'll also discuss how to combine these methods to get a comprehensive view of a stock's potential, ensuring you make informed, confident investment choices.

The Concept of Intrinsic Value: What is a Stock Really Worth?

At the heart of stock valuation is the concept of intrinsic value—the true, underlying value of a stock based on its fundamentals. Intrinsic value is independent of the stock's current market price, which can fluctuate due to investor sentiment, market conditions, or short-term events. As a Minimalistic Entrepreneur, your goal is to identify stocks that are trading below their intrinsic value, providing an opportunity to buy at a discount and benefit from future price appreciation.

Fundamental Analysis: The Foundation of Valuation

Fundamental analysis is a method of evaluating a stock by examining the financial health, performance, and growth prospects of the company behind it. This approach is rooted in the belief that a stock's price will eventually reflect its true value based on the company's earnings, assets, and overall financial condition.

Here's how to approach fundamental analysis:

1. Analyzing Financial Statements:

The first step in fundamental analysis is to dive into a company's financial statements. These documents provide a wealth of information about the company's profitability, financial stability, and potential for growth.

- Income Statement: The income statement, or profit and loss statement, shows the company's revenues, expenses, and profits over a specific period. Key metrics to look at include revenue growth, net income, and profit margins. Consistent revenue growth and strong profit margins are indicators of a healthy, growing company.

- Balance Sheet: The balance sheet provides a snapshot of the company's assets, liabilities, and shareholders' equity at a given point in time. It helps you assess the company's financial strength and its ability to meet short-term and long-term obligations. Pay attention to the company's debt levels, liquidity (current assets vs. current liabilities), and book value (total assets minus total liabilities).

- Cash Flow Statement: The cash flow statement tracks the flow of cash in and out of the company, revealing how well the company manages its cash. Positive cash flow from operations is a good sign that the company generates enough cash to sustain its operations and invest in growth. Free cash flow (operating cash flow minus capital expenditures) is particularly important, as it represents the cash available to shareholders after the company has reinvested in its business.

2. Earnings Per Share (EPS):

Earnings Per Share (EPS) is a key indicator of a company's profitability, calculated by dividing net income by the number of outstanding shares. A growing EPS over time suggests that the company is successfully increasing its profits and providing greater returns to shareholders.

When evaluating EPS, it's important to consider both the absolute value and the growth rate. A high EPS growth rate indicates that the company is expanding its earnings at a rapid pace, which can drive future stock price appreciation. However, also compare the EPS growth rate to industry peers to ensure that the company is outperforming its competitors.

3. Price-to-Earnings (P/E) Ratio:

The Price-to-Earnings (P/E) ratio is one of the most widely used valuation metrics. It compares the stock's current price to its earnings per share, providing insight into how much investors are willing to pay for each rupee of earnings.

- High P/E Ratio: A high P/E ratio may indicate that the stock is overvalued, or it could suggest that investors expect strong future growth. Growth stocks typically have higher P/E ratios due to their potential for rapid earnings growth.

- Low P/E Ratio: A low P/E ratio may indicate that the stock is undervalued or that the market has low expectations for the company's future growth. Value investors often seek out stocks with low P/E ratios, believing that they are buying at a discount.

It's important to compare the P/E ratio to the industry average and the broader market to get a sense of whether the stock is fairly valued. Additionally, consider the company's growth prospects—sometimes a high P/E ratio is justified if the company is expected to grow earnings significantly in the future.

4. Dividend Yield and Payout Ratio:

For dividend-paying stocks, the dividend yield is an important metric to consider. It represents the annual dividend payment as a percentage of the stock's current price. A higher dividend yield may be attractive to income-focused investors, but it's important to ensure that the company can sustain its dividend payments.

The payout ratio, which is the percentage of earnings paid out as dividends, helps assess the sustainability of the dividend. A high payout ratio may indicate that the company is returning most of its earnings to shareholders, which could limit its ability to reinvest in growth. Conversely, a low payout ratio suggests that the company retains more earnings for reinvestment, which could drive future growth.

5. Return on Equity (ROE) and Return on Assets (ROA):

Return on Equity (ROE) measures how effectively a company uses shareholders' equity to generate profits, while Return on Assets (ROA) measures how efficiently the company uses its assets to generate profits.

- High ROE: A high ROE indicates that the company is effectively using shareholders' equity to generate returns. However, be cautious of companies with extremely high ROE driven by high levels of debt, as this can increase financial risk.

- High ROA: A high ROA suggests that the company is efficient in using its assets to generate profits. This is particularly important in asset-heavy industries, where efficient use of assets can significantly impact profitability.

6. Debt-to-Equity Ratio:

The Debt-to-Equity (D/E) ratio is a measure of a company's financial leverage, calculated by dividing its total liabilities by shareholders' equity. A higher D/E ratio indicates that the company relies more on debt to finance its operations, which can increase financial risk.

For the Minimalistic Entrepreneur, a lower D/E ratio may indicate a safer investment, especially in uncertain economic times. However, some industries, such as utilities and real estate, typically operate with higher D/E ratios due to the capital-intensive nature of their businesses. It's important to consider the industry context when evaluating the D/E ratio.

Technical Analysis: Timing Your Entry and Exit

While fundamental analysis focuses on a company's intrinsic value, technical analysis is concerned with the stock's price movements and trading patterns. This approach is particularly useful for identifying the best times to buy or sell a stock based on market trends and investor behavior.

Here's how to approach technical analysis:

1. Understanding Stock Charts:

Stock charts visually represent a stock's price movements over time. They can help you identify trends, support and resistance levels, and potential entry and exit points.

- Line Charts: Line charts are the simplest type of stock chart, showing the closing prices of a stock over a specific period. They provide a clear view of the stock's price trend but lack detailed information about intraday price movements.

- Candlestick Charts: Candlestick charts provide more detailed information about a stock's price movements within a given period, including the opening, closing, high, and low prices. Each "candlestick" on the chart represents one period of trading (e.g., a day or a week) and is color-coded to indicate whether the price increased (typically shown in green) or decreased (typically shown in red).

- Bar Charts: Bar charts also show the opening, closing, high, and low prices, but use vertical bars instead of candlesticks. They provide similar information to candlestick charts but may be easier to read for some investors.

2. Identifying Trends:

One of the key principles of technical analysis is that stock prices tend to move in trends. Identifying these trends can help you make informed decisions about when to enter or exit a position.

- Uptrend: An uptrend is characterized by a series of higher highs and higher lows, indicating that the stock's price is generally moving upward. In an uptrend, buying on pullbacks (temporary price declines) can be a profitable strategy.

- Downtrend: A downtrend is characterized by a series of lower highs and lower lows, indicating that the stock's price is generally moving downward. In a downtrend, selling or shorting the stock may be more appropriate.

- Sideways Trend: A sideways trend occurs when the stock's price moves within a relatively narrow range, without a clear upward or downward direction. In this case, it may be best to wait for a breakout (a strong move above or below the range) before making a decision.

3. Support and Resistance Levels:

Support and resistance levels are key concepts in technical analysis that refer to price levels at which a stock tends to stop and reverse direction.

- Support Level: A support level is a price point where the stock tends to find buying interest, preventing it from falling further. It's considered a "floor" that the stock price has difficulty breaking through. If the stock price falls to a support level, it may be a good buying opportunity, as the price is likely to rebound.

- Resistance Level: A resistance level is a price point where the stock tends to face selling pressure, preventing it from rising further. It's considered a "ceiling" that the stock price has difficulty breaking through. If the stock price rises to a resistance level, it may be a good selling opportunity, as the price is likely to pull back. By identifying these levels, you can make more informed decisions about when to buy or sell a stock.

4. Moving Averages:

Moving averages are commonly used technical indicators that smooth out price data to create a trend-following indicator. They help identify the direction of the trend and potential reversals.

- Simple Moving Average (SMA): The SMA is calculated by averaging the closing prices of a stock over a specific period (e.g., 50 days, 200 days). A rising SMA indicates an uptrend, while a falling SMA indicates a downtrend.

- Exponential Moving Average (EMA): The EMA gives more weight to recent prices, making it more responsive to price changes. It's useful for identifying shorter-term trends and potential reversals.

Moving averages can also be used in conjunction with other indicators to confirm trends or identify potential buy or sell signals. For example, a common strategy is to look for a "golden cross" (when the short-term moving average crosses above the long-term moving average) as a buy signal, and a "death cross" (when the short-term moving average crosses below the long-term moving average) as a sell signal.

5. Relative Strength Index (RSI):

The Relative Strength Index (RSI) is a momentum oscillator that measures the speed and change of price movements. It ranges from 0 to 100 and is used to identify overbought or oversold conditions in a stock.

- Overbought: When the RSI is above 70, the stock may be considered overbought, meaning it has risen too quickly and may be due for a pullback.

- Oversold: When the RSI is below 30, the stock may be considered oversold, meaning it has fallen too quickly and may be due for a rebound.

The RSI can be a helpful tool for timing your entry and exit points, especially when used in conjunction with other indicators.

6. Volume Analysis:

Volume refers to the number of shares traded during a specific period. Analyzing volume can provide insights into the strength of a price movement or trend.

- High Volume: A price movement accompanied by high volume is generally considered more significant and likely to continue. For example, if a stock breaks through a resistance level on high volume, it's a strong indication that the breakout is valid.

- Low Volume: A price movement on low volume may indicate a lack of conviction, suggesting that the trend may not be sustainable. For example, if a stock rises on low volume, it could be a sign of weak buying interest and a potential reversal.

Combining Fundamental and Technical Analysis

While fundamental and technical analysis are often viewed as separate approaches, combining them can provide a more comprehensive view of a stock's potential. Here's how you can integrate both methods into your investment strategy:

1. Start with Fundamental Analysis:

Begin by evaluating the company's fundamentals to determine whether it's a strong, well-managed business with growth potential. Look for companies with solid financials, competitive advantages, and a reasonable valuation. This will help you identify stocks that are worth considering for your portfolio.

2. Use Technical Analysis for Timing:

Once you've identified a fundamentally strong stock, use technical analysis to determine the best time to buy or sell. Look for trends, support and resistance levels, and other technical indicators to help you time your entry and exit points. This can help you avoid buying at a peak or selling at a low.

3. Monitor Both Fundamentals and Technicals:

Continuously monitor both the fundamental and technical aspects of your investments. Stay informed about the company's financial performance, industry developments, and market trends, while also keeping an eye on the stock's price movements and trading patterns. This holistic approach will help you make more informed and confident decisions.

Conclusion: Mastering the Art of Valuation

Understanding stock valuation methods is a critical skill for any Minimalistic Entrepreneur. By combining fundamental and technical analysis, you can gain a deeper insight into the true value of a stock and make more informed investment decisions. Remember, the goal is not to find the perfect stock at the perfect time—such precision is impossible. Instead, focus on building a well-researched, diversified portfolio that aligns with your long-term financial goals.

Investing is both an art and a science, requiring continuous learning, discipline, and a commitment to your strategy. By mastering valuation methods, you're equipping yourself with the tools to navigate the stock market confidently and build lasting wealth as a Minimalistic Entrepreneur. Keep honing your skills, stay informed, and remember that every investment decision brings you one step closer to financial freedom.

CHAPTER FIVE

BUILDING YOUR INVESTMENT STRATEGY

Fundamental Analysis vs. Technical Analysis

As you continue your journey as a Minimalistic Entrepreneur in the stock market, one of the key decisions you'll face is choosing your approach to analyzing and selecting stocks. Two of the most widely used methods in the world of investing are fundamental analysis and technical analysis. Each has its own merits, and understanding the strengths and weaknesses of both will empower you to craft a strategy that aligns with your goals, risk tolerance, and investment style.

In this chapter, we'll delve into the differences between fundamental and technical analysis, explore when and how to use each method, and discuss how you can combine them to create a well-rounded investment strategy. The aim is not just to understand these approaches but to use them as tools that help you make informed decisions and stay committed to your long-term financial goals.

Fundamental Analysis: The Long-Term Perspective

Fundamental analysis is all about understanding the intrinsic value of a stock. It's rooted in the belief that the true worth of a stock is determined by the financial health, performance, and future prospects of the company behind it. Investors who use fundamental analysis look at a company's financial statements, management quality, industry position, and economic factors to gauge its potential for long-term growth and profitability.

Key Elements of Fundamental Analysis

1. Financial Health:

At the core of fundamental analysis is the evaluation of a company's financial health. This involves analyzing key financial statements, such as the income statement, balance sheet, and cash flow statement, to assess the company's profitability, stability, and ability to generate cash.

- Revenue and Earnings Growth: Consistent growth in revenue and earnings is a positive sign that the company is expanding its operations and increasing profitability. Look for companies with a track record of steady growth over several years.

- Profit Margins: Profit margins, including gross margin, operating margin, and net margin, indicate how efficiently a company is managing its costs relative to its revenues. Higher margins suggest better management efficiency and profitability.

- Debt Levels: A company's debt levels can significantly impact its financial stability. Evaluate the debt-to-equity ratio to understand how much debt the company is using to finance its operations. Lower debt levels generally indicate lower financial risk.

2. Management Quality:

The success of a company often depends on the quality of its management team. Strong leadership, a clear strategic vision, and a commitment to creating shareholder value are all signs of a competent management team.

- Experience and Track Record: Research the backgrounds of key executives, including the CEO, CFO, and board members. A management team with a proven track record of success in the industry is more likely to steer the company toward growth and profitability.

- Corporate Governance: Good corporate governance practices, such as transparency, accountability, and ethical behavior, are essential for building trust with shareholders. Companies with strong governance are more likely to make decisions that align with shareholder interests.

3. Industry and Market Position:

A company's position within its industry can significantly impact its long-term prospects. Companies that dominate their industries or have a unique competitive advantage are better positioned to weather economic downturns and capitalize on growth opportunities.

- Market Share: Companies with a large market share often have competitive advantages, such as economies of scale, brand recognition, or a loyal customer base. These advantages can help them maintain profitability even in challenging market conditions.

- Industry Growth: Invest in industries with strong growth potential, driven by factors such as technological advancements, demographic trends, or regulatory changes. For example, the technology sector in India has seen significant growth due to the global demand for digital transformation services.

4. Valuation Metrics:

Fundamental analysis involves assessing whether a stock is fairly valued based on its financial performance and growth prospects. Key valuation metrics include the Price-to-Earnings (P/E) ratio, Price-to-Book (P/B) ratio, and Dividend Yield.

- P/E Ratio: The P/E ratio compares the stock's current price to its earnings per share, providing insight into how much investors are willing to pay for each rupee of earnings. A lower P/E ratio may indicate that the stock is undervalued, while a higher P/E ratio may suggest that investors expect strong future growth.

- P/B Ratio: The P/B ratio compares the stock's market price to its book value (assets minus liabilities). A lower P/B ratio may indicate that the stock is trading at a discount to its intrinsic value.

- Dividend Yield: For dividend-paying stocks, the dividend yield is an important metric to consider. It represents the annual dividend payment as a percentage of the stock's current price. A higher dividend yield may be attractive to income-focused investors.

When to Use Fundamental Analysis

Fundamental analysis is best suited for investors with a long-term perspective who are interested in identifying undervalued stocks and holding them for extended periods. It's particularly effective for value investors who seek to buy quality companies at a discount and wait for the market to recognize their true value.

For the Minimalistic Entrepreneur, fundamental analysis is a powerful tool for building a portfolio of strong, financially stable companies that are likely to deliver consistent returns over time. It's about focusing on the underlying business and its ability to generate sustainable profits, rather than getting caught up in short-term market fluctuations.

Technical Analysis: The Short-Term Perspective

While fundamental analysis focuses on the intrinsic value of a stock, technical analysis is concerned with the stock's price movements and trading patterns. It's based on the belief that all relevant information is already reflected in the stock's price, and that by analyzing past price movements, investors can predict future price trends.

Key Elements of Technical Analysis

1. Price Trends:

One of the core principles of technical analysis is that stock prices tend to move in trends. Identifying these trends can help you determine the direction of the market and make informed decisions about when to buy or sell.

- Uptrend: An uptrend is characterized by a series of higher highs and higher lows, indicating that the stock's price is generally moving upward. Investors often look to buy stocks during an uptrend, as the momentum is positive.

- Downtrend: A downtrend is characterized by a series of lower highs and lower lows, indicating that the stock's price is generally moving downward. Investors may look to sell or short stocks during a downtrend, as the momentum is negative.

- Sideways Trend: A sideways trend occurs when the stock's price moves within a relatively narrow range, without a clear upward or downward direction. In this case, it may be best to wait for a breakout before making a decision.

2. Support and Resistance Levels:

Support and resistance levels are key concepts in technical analysis that refer to price levels at which a stock tends to stop and reverse direction.

- Support Level: A support level is a price point where the stock tends to find buying interest, preventing it from falling further. If the stock price falls to a support level, it may be a good buying opportunity.

- Resistance Level: A resistance level is a price point where the stock tends to face selling pressure, preventing it from rising further. If the stock price rises to a resistance level, it may be a good selling opportunity.

3. Moving Averages:

Moving averages are commonly used technical indicators that smooth out price data to create a trend-following indicator. They help identify the direction of the trend and potential reversals.

- Simple Moving Average (SMA): The SMA is calculated by averaging the closing prices of a stock over a specific period (e.g., 50 days, 200 days). A rising SMA indicates an uptrend, while a falling SMA indicates a downtrend.

- Exponential Moving Average (EMA): The EMA gives more weight to recent prices, making it more responsive to price changes. It's useful for identifying shorter-term trends and potential reversals.

4. Relative Strength Index (RSI):

The Relative Strength Index (RSI) is a momentum oscillator that measures the speed and change of price movements. It ranges from 0 to 100 and is used to identify overbought or oversold conditions in a stock.

- Overbought: When the RSI is above 70, the stock may be considered overbought, meaning it has risen too quickly and may be due for a pullback.

- Oversold: When the RSI is below 30, the stock may be considered oversold, meaning it has fallen too quickly and may be due for a rebound.

5. Volume Analysis:

Volume refers to the number of shares traded during a specific period. Analyzing volume can provide insights into the strength of a price movement or trend.

- High Volume: A price movement accompanied by high volume is generally considered more significant and likely to continue.

- Low Volume: A price movement on low volume may indicate a lack of conviction, suggesting that the trend may not be sustainable.

When to Use Technical Analysis

Technical analysis is particularly useful for short-term traders who aim to capitalize on price movements over days, weeks, or months. It's also valuable for identifying entry and exit points, even for long-term investors who want to optimize their purchase and sale decisions.

For the Minimalistic Entrepreneur, technical analysis can complement your long-term investment strategy by helping you time your trades more effectively. While your primary focus may be on the company's fundamentals, technical analysis can provide additional insights into market sentiment and potential price trends.

Combining Fundamental and Technical Analysis: The Best of Both Worlds

While fundamental and technical analysis are often viewed as distinct approaches, they can be combined to create a more comprehensive investment strategy. Here's how you can integrate both methods:

1. Start with Fundamental Analysis:

Begin by identifying fundamentally strong companies with solid financials, competitive advantages, and growth potential. This will help you build a portfolio of quality stocks that are likely to deliver consistent returns over the long term.

2. Use Technical Analysis for Timing:

Once you've identified a fundamentally strong stock, use technical analysis to determine the best time to buy or sell. Look for trends, support and resistance levels, and other technical indicators to help you time your entry and exit points. This can help you avoid buying at a peak or selling at a low.

3. Monitor Both Fundamentals and Technicals:

Continuously monitor both the fundamental and technical aspects of your investments. Stay informed about the company's financial performance, industry developments, and market trends, while also keeping an eye on the stock's price movements and trading patterns. This holistic approach will help you make more informed and confident decisions.

Conclusion: Crafting Your Unique Investment Strategy

As a Minimalistic Entrepreneur, your goal is to build a portfolio that aligns with your financial goals while managing risk effectively. Whether you choose to focus on fundamental analysis, technical analysis, or a combination of both, the key is to stay disciplined, stay informed, and stay committed to your strategy.

Remember, there's no one-size-fits-all approach to investing. Your strategy should reflect your individual goals, risk tolerance, and time horizon. By understanding and applying both fundamental and technical analysis, you're equipping yourself with the tools to navigate the stock market confidently and build lasting wealth. Keep honing your skills, stay informed, and trust in your ability to make smart, informed investment decisions.

Value Investing for the Minimalistic Entrepreneur

Value investing is more than just a strategy; it's a philosophy that has stood the test of time. Pioneered by legendary investors like Benjamin Graham and Warren Buffett, value investing is based on the simple principle of buying stocks that are undervalued by the market. For the Minimalistic Entrepreneur, value investing offers a disciplined approach to building wealth by focusing on quality companies trading at a discount to their intrinsic value. In this chapter, we'll explore the core concepts of value investing, how to identify undervalued stocks, and how to apply this strategy to your portfolio for long-term success.

The Essence of Value Investing: Buy Low, Hold High

At its core, value investing is about finding diamonds in the rough—companies that are fundamentally strong but are trading below their intrinsic value due to temporary market misjudgments. The idea is to buy these stocks when they are undervalued and hold them until the market realizes their true worth, leading to price appreciation. Unlike short-term trading, value investing requires patience, discipline, and a long-term perspective.

Why Value Investing?

Value investing is particularly appealing for the Minimalistic Entrepreneur for several reasons:

1. Lower Risk: By focusing on undervalued stocks, you're essentially buying at a discount, which provides a margin of safety. This margin helps protect your investment from downside risk, as you're less likely to experience significant losses if the stock is already trading below its intrinsic value.

2. Long-Term Focus: Value investing aligns with the long-term goals of the Minimalistic Entrepreneur. Instead of chasing short-term gains, you're building a portfolio that will grow steadily over time, benefiting from the compounding effect of reinvested dividends and capital appreciation.

3. Opportunities in Market Inefficiencies: Markets are not always rational. Emotional reactions, herd behavior, and short-term market noise can lead to mispricing of stocks. Value investors take advantage of these inefficiencies by buying stocks that are temporarily out of favor but have strong underlying fundamentals.

The Principles of Value Investing

Value investing is built on several key principles that guide the selection of stocks and the management of a value-focused portfolio:

1. Intrinsic Value:

The concept of intrinsic value is central to value investing. Intrinsic value refers to the true, underlying worth of a company, independent of its current market price. It's determined by analyzing the company's financials, growth prospects, and economic environment.

Calculating intrinsic value requires a thorough understanding of a company's fundamentals, including its revenue, earnings, cash flow, and assets. While there are various methods to estimate intrinsic value, such as Discounted Cash Flow (DCF) analysis, the key is to determine whether a stock is trading below its intrinsic value, indicating a buying opportunity.

2. Margin of Safety:

The margin of safety is a cushion that protects you from downside risk. It represents the difference between a stock's intrinsic value and its current market price. The larger the margin of safety, the less risk you take on when buying the stock.

For example, if you estimate a company's intrinsic value to be ₹ 500 per share and the stock is currently trading at ₹350, the margin of safety is ₹150 per share, or 30%. This margin provides protection against unforeseen events, such as market downturns or negative news, that could temporarily affect the stock's price.

3. Patience and Discipline:

Value investing requires a patient and disciplined approach. It's not about reacting to short-term market movements or chasing the latest trends. Instead, value investors are willing to wait for the market to recognize the true value of their holdings, even if it takes years.

This long-term perspective is crucial for the Minimalistic Entrepreneur, who values steady, sustainable growth over quick profits. By staying focused on the underlying value of your investments, you can avoid the pitfalls of emotional trading and market speculation.

How to Identify Undervalued Stocks

Identifying undervalued stocks is both an art and a science. It involves a combination of quantitative analysis, qualitative assessment, and a deep understanding of the market. Here are the steps you can take to find value opportunities in the stock market:

1. Screening for Value Stocks:

The first step in identifying undervalued stocks is to use stock screeners to filter potential candidates. Stock screeners allow you to set specific criteria, such as low P/E ratio, high dividend yield, or low P/B ratio, to narrow down the list of stocks that may be undervalued.

Common criteria for screening value stocks include:

- Low P/E Ratio: A low Price-to-Earnings ratio compared to industry peers or the market average may indicate that the stock is undervalued.

- High Dividend Yield: Stocks with a high dividend yield relative to their peers may be undervalued, especially if the company has a history of maintaining or increasing dividends.

- Low P/B Ratio: A low Price-to-Book ratio suggests that the stock is trading at a discount to its book value, which can be a sign of undervaluation.

2. Analyzing Financial Health:

Once you've identified potential value stocks, the next step is to analyze the company's financial health. This involves reviewing key financial statements, such as the income statement, balance sheet, and cash flow statement, to assess the company's profitability, stability, and growth potential.

- Revenue and Earnings Growth: Look for companies with consistent revenue and earnings growth over the past several years. Steady growth indicates a strong business model and increasing demand for the company's products or services.

- Profit Margins: Analyze the company's profit margins to assess its efficiency in managing costs and generating profits. Higher margins suggest better management efficiency and profitability.

- Debt Levels: Evaluate the company's debt-to-equity ratio to understand its financial leverage. Companies with lower debt levels are generally safer investments, especially in economic downturns.

3. Assessing Competitive Advantage:

A key aspect of value investing is identifying companies with a durable competitive advantage, often referred to as an "economic moat." A competitive advantage allows a company to maintain its market position and profitability over the long term, even in the face of competition.

- Brand Strength: Companies with strong brand recognition and customer loyalty often have a competitive edge. Brands like Tata, Infosys, and Maruti Suzuki are examples of companies with a strong presence in their respective industries.

- Cost Leadership: Companies that can produce goods or services at a lower cost than competitors have a significant advantage. This cost leadership allows them to maintain profitability even in highly competitive markets.

- Intellectual Property: Patents, trademarks, and proprietary technology can provide a significant competitive advantage, allowing companies to protect their market position and charge premium prices.

4. Valuation Metrics:

To determine whether a stock is undervalued, you'll need to assess its valuation using various metrics. Some of the most commonly used valuation metrics in value investing include:

- Price-to-Earnings (P/E) Ratio: The P/E ratio compares the stock's current price to its earnings per share. A lower P/E ratio compared to industry peers or the market average may indicate that the stock is undervalued.

- Price-to-Book (P/B) Ratio: The P/B ratio compares the stock's market price to its book value. A lower P/B ratio suggests that the stock is trading at a discount to its book value, which can be a sign of undervaluation.

- Dividend Yield: For dividend-paying stocks, the dividend yield is an important metric to consider. A higher dividend yield relative to peers may indicate that the stock is undervalued, especially if the company has a history of maintaining or increasing dividends.

5. Qualitative Assessment:

In addition to quantitative analysis, qualitative factors also play a crucial role in identifying undervalued stocks. This involves assessing the company's management quality, industry position, and growth prospects.

- Management Quality: Research the background and experience of the company's key executives, including the CEO, CFO, and board members. A strong leadership team with a proven track record of success is more likely to steer the company toward growth and profitability.

- Industry Position: Consider the company's position within its industry. Companies that dominate their industries or have a unique competitive advantage are better positioned to weather economic downturns and capitalize on growth opportunities.

- Growth Prospects: Evaluate the company's long-term growth prospects, including potential market expansion, product innovation, and strategic acquisitions. Companies with strong growth prospects are more likely to deliver long-term value to shareholders.

The Art of Patience: Holding for the Long Term

One of the defining characteristics of value investing is the emphasis on patience. Unlike short-term trading, which focuses on quick gains, value investing requires a long-term perspective. Once you've identified an undervalued stock and made your investment, the key is to hold on to it until the market recognizes its true value.

Here's how to cultivate the patience required for successful value investing:

1. Stay Focused on Fundamentals:

The stock market can be volatile, with prices fluctuating daily based on news, economic data, and investor sentiment. As a value investor, it's important to stay focused on the underlying fundamentals of your investments rather than getting caught up in short-term market noise.

If the company's fundamentals remain strong and its growth prospects are intact, there's no need to panic during market downturns. In fact, market corrections can provide opportunities to buy more shares at an even greater discount.

2. Avoid Emotional Decision-Making:

Emotions can be the enemy of successful investing. Fear, greed, and impatience can lead to impulsive decisions that undermine your long-term strategy. Value investing requires a disciplined approach, where decisions are based on careful analysis rather than emotional reactions.

If you find yourself getting anxious about market fluctuations, remind yourself of the reasons you invested in the stock in the first place. Revisit your research, review the company's financials, and assess whether anything has fundamentally changed. If not, stay the course and trust in your analysis.

3. Reinvest Dividends:

One of the benefits of value investing is the potential for dividend income. Reinvesting dividends back into your portfolio can accelerate the compounding effect, leading to greater wealth accumulation over time.

By reinvesting dividends, you're essentially buying more shares at a discount, which can enhance your overall returns when the stock's price eventually appreciates. Many brokerage platforms offer automatic dividend reinvestment plans (DRIPs), making it easy to reinvest dividends without having to manually purchase additional shares.

4. Review and Reassess Periodically:

While value investing requires patience, it's also important to periodically review and reassess your portfolio. Over time, the market's perception of a company may change, or new information may come to light that affects its intrinsic value.

Set aside time to review your investments on a regular basis, such as quarterly or annually. During these reviews, reassess the company's financial health, growth prospects, and valuation. If a stock has reached or exceeded its intrinsic value, it may be time to consider selling and reallocating your capital to other undervalued opportunities.

Conclusion: Value Investing as a Path to Wealth

Value investing is a time-tested strategy that aligns perfectly with the goals of the Minimalistic Entrepreneur. By focusing on quality companies that are trading at a discount to their intrinsic value, you can build a portfolio that provides both stability and growth potential. The principles of value investing—intrinsic value, margin of safety, patience, and discipline—are essential tools that will guide you on your journey to financial independence.

Remember, value investing is not about chasing quick gains or reacting to short-term market movements. It's about making informed, rational decisions based on careful analysis and a deep understanding of the companies you invest in. By staying committed to the principles of value investing, you're not just buying stocks—you're building wealth, one undervalued opportunity at a time.

As you continue to hone your skills as a value investor, keep in mind that the stock market is a long-term game. Success doesn't happen overnight, but with patience, discipline, and a focus on intrinsic value, you can achieve the financial freedom and lasting wealth that you seek as a Minimalistic Entrepreneur.

Creating a Diversified Portfolio

As a Minimalistic Entrepreneur, one of your key objectives is to build a portfolio that not only aligns with your financial goals but also mitigates risks. The stock market is inherently unpredictable, and while you can never eliminate risk entirely, you can certainly manage it. Diversification is the cornerstone of risk management in investing. It's a strategy that spreads your investments across different asset classes, sectors, and geographies to reduce the impact of any single investment's poor performance on your overall portfolio.

In this chapter, we'll dive deep into the principles of diversification, how to create a diversified portfolio, and the benefits and challenges of maintaining diversification over time. By the end of this chapter, you'll have a clear understanding of how to construct a portfolio that balances risk and return, giving you the confidence to navigate the stock market with a well-rounded strategy.

The Importance of Diversification: Don't Put All Your Eggs in One Basket

Diversification is based on a simple but powerful idea: by spreading your investments across a variety of assets, you reduce the likelihood that a single bad investment will significantly harm your portfolio. This strategy doesn't just involve picking multiple stocks—it's about choosing a mix of investments that don't move in tandem, so that when one part of your portfolio underperforms, another part may do well.

Why Diversification Matters

1. Reduces Risk: The primary benefit of diversification is risk reduction. By investing in a variety of assets, you spread your exposure and reduce the impact of any one investment's poor performance. If one sector or asset class experiences a downturn, the losses may be offset by gains in another area of your portfolio.

2. Enhances Stability: A diversified portfolio tends to be more stable, as it's less vulnerable to market volatility. This stability is particularly important for the Minimalistic Entrepreneur, who seeks steady, long-term

growth rather than chasing short-term gains.

3. Opportunities for Growth: Diversification also opens up opportunities for growth by allowing you to invest in different sectors, asset classes, and geographies. This broader exposure can lead to higher returns over time, especially when certain parts of your portfolio outperform expectations.

Core Principles of Diversification

Building a diversified portfolio involves more than just buying a bunch of different stocks. To create an effective diversification strategy, you need to understand the following core principles:

1. Asset Allocation:

Asset allocation is the process of dividing your investments among different asset classes, such as stocks, bonds, real estate, and cash. The goal is to create a mix that aligns with your risk tolerance, financial goals, and time horizon.

- Stocks: Stocks are often the primary component of a growth-oriented portfolio. They offer the potential for high returns but come with higher risk and volatility. Within the stock category, you can further diversify by investing in different sectors (e.g., technology, healthcare, consumer goods) and market capitalizations (e.g., large-cap, mid-cap, small-cap).

- Bonds: Bonds are generally considered lower-risk investments compared to stocks. They provide regular income through interest payments and are less volatile. Bonds can help stabilize your portfolio, especially during periods of stock market downturns.

- Real Estate: Real estate investments, including Real Estate Investment Trusts (REITs), provide exposure to the property market. Real estate can offer a steady income through rental yields and potential for capital appreciation. It also adds a layer of diversification, as real estate often behaves differently from stocks and bonds.

- Cash and Cash Equivalents: Holding cash or cash equivalents (such as money market funds) provides liquidity and safety. While cash typically earns lower returns, it's useful for meeting short-term financial needs and taking advantage of investment opportunities as they arise.

Your asset allocation should reflect your personal financial situation, including your age, risk tolerance, and investment goals. For example, a younger investor with a long time horizon might allocate a higher percentage of their portfolio to stocks, while an older investor nearing retirement might prioritize bonds and cash to preserve capital.

2. *Sector Diversification:*

Within your stock investments, it's important to diversify across different sectors of the economy. Sectors are groups of companies that operate in the same industry, such as technology, healthcare, finance, or energy. Each sector has its own unique characteristics and responds differently to economic conditions.

- Technology: The technology sector includes companies involved in software, hardware, telecommunications, and internet services. This sector tends to be growth-oriented but can be volatile due to rapid innovation and competition.

- Healthcare: The healthcare sector includes pharmaceutical companies, healthcare providers, and biotechnology firms. This sector is often seen as defensive, as healthcare services are essential regardless of economic conditions.

- Finance: The finance sector includes banks, insurance companies, and investment firms. This sector is sensitive to interest rates and economic cycles, but it also offers opportunities for steady income through dividends.

- Consumer Goods: The consumer goods sector includes companies that produce essential and non-essential products, such as food, beverages, clothing, and electronics. This sector is driven by consumer spending and can provide stability during economic downturns.

- Energy: The energy sector includes companies involved in the production and distribution of energy, such as oil, gas, and renewable energy firms. This sector is influenced by global energy demand and commodity prices.

By diversifying across sectors, you reduce the risk of being overly exposed to any one industry. For example, if the technology sector experiences a downturn, your losses may be offset by gains in the healthcare or consumer goods sectors.

3. *Geographical Diversification:*

Geographical diversification involves spreading your investments across different regions and countries. This strategy helps reduce the risk associated with economic or political instability in any one country.

- Domestic Markets: Investing in domestic markets (e.g., the Indian stock market) provides exposure to companies that operate in your home country. These investments are often more familiar and may be subject to local economic conditions.

- International Markets: Investing in international markets provides exposure to global growth opportunities and helps mitigate the risk of being overly reliant on a single country's economy. For example, you might invest in U.S. tech companies, European industrial firms, or emerging market stocks in Asia.

- Emerging Markets: Emerging markets are countries with developing economies, such as India, China, Brazil, and South Africa. These markets offer higher growth potential but also come with higher risk due to economic volatility and political instability.

Geographical diversification allows you to benefit from growth in different parts of the world while reducing the impact of economic downturns in any one region.

4. Investment Styles:

Diversifying by investment style involves balancing growth and value stocks within your portfolio. Growth stocks are companies that are expected to grow at an above-average rate, while value stocks are companies that are trading below their intrinsic value.

- Growth Investing: Growth stocks are typically found in sectors like technology, healthcare, and consumer discretionary. These stocks offer high potential returns but also come with higher risk due to their reliance on future growth expectations.

- Value Investing: Value stocks are often found in sectors like finance, utilities, and consumer staples. These stocks may be undervalued by the market and offer a margin of safety, providing stability and potential for price appreciation.

By including both growth and value stocks in your portfolio, you can balance the potential for high returns with the stability of more conservative investments.

Constructing Your Diversified Portfolio

Now that you understand the principles of diversification, it's time to put them into practice by constructing your portfolio. Here's a step-by-step guide to building a diversified portfolio that aligns with your financial goals:

1. Assess Your Risk Tolerance:

Before you start selecting investments, it's important to assess your risk tolerance. Risk tolerance refers to your ability and willingness to endure fluctuations in the value of your investments. Factors that influence risk tolerance include your age, financial situation, investment goals, and time horizon.

- Conservative Risk Tolerance: If you have a low risk tolerance, you may prefer a more conservative portfolio with a higher allocation to bonds and cash. This approach prioritizes capital preservation over high returns.

- Moderate Risk Tolerance: If you have a moderate risk tolerance, you may choose a balanced portfolio with a mix of stocks, bonds, and other assets. This approach aims for steady growth with some protection against volatility.

- Aggressive Risk Tolerance: If you have a high risk tolerance, you may prefer a more aggressive portfolio with a higher allocation to stocks and growth-oriented investments. This approach seeks higher returns but comes with increased volatility.

2. Determine Your Asset Allocation:

Based on your risk tolerance and financial goals, determine the appropriate asset allocation for your portfolio. Your asset allocation should reflect your investment horizon and the level of risk you're comfortable taking.

For example, a young investor with a long time horizon and high risk tolerance might allocate 70% of their portfolio to stocks, 20% to bonds, and 10% to real estate. An older investor nearing retirement with a conservative risk tolerance might allocate 40% to stocks, 40% to bonds, and 20% to cash.

3. Select Your Investments:

Once you've determined your asset allocation, select investments that fit within each asset class. Consider the following when selecting investments:

- Stock Selection: Diversify your stock investments across different sectors, market capitalizations, and geographical regions. Include a mix of growth and value stocks to balance potential returns with stability.

- Bond Selection: Choose bonds with varying maturities and credit ratings to reduce interest rate and credit risk. Consider including both government and corporate bonds in your portfolio for additional diversification.

- Real Estate: If you're investing in real estate, consider a mix of direct property investments and REITs to gain exposure to different segments of the property market.

- Cash and Cash Equivalents: Hold cash in high-yield savings accounts or money market funds to earn interest while maintaining liquidity.

4. Regularly Rebalance Your Portfolio:

Over time, the value of your investments will fluctuate, causing your asset allocation to drift from its original target. Regularly rebalancing your portfolio involves adjusting your investments to bring your asset allocation back in line with your goals.

For example, if your stock investments have grown significantly, you may need to sell some stocks and buy bonds or other assets to restore your desired asset allocation. Rebalancing helps maintain your risk profile and ensures that your portfolio remains aligned with your financial goals.

5. Monitor and Adjust as Needed:

While diversification helps reduce risk, it's important to monitor your portfolio regularly and adjust your strategy as needed. Keep an eye on changes in your financial situation, investment goals, and market conditions, and make adjustments to your portfolio accordingly.

For example, if you're approaching retirement, you may want to gradually shift your portfolio toward more conservative investments to preserve capital. Conversely, if you experience a windfall, such as an inheritance or bonus, you may choose to increase your exposure to growth-oriented investments.

Challenges and Considerations in Diversification

While diversification is a powerful strategy, it's not without its challenges. Here are some considerations to keep in mind:

1. Over-Diversification:

It's possible to over-diversify your portfolio by holding too many investments. Over-diversification can dilute your returns and make it difficult to manage your portfolio effectively. Aim for a balanced approach where you have enough diversification to reduce risk but not so much that your portfolio becomes unmanageable.

2. Costs and Fees:

Diversifying across multiple asset classes, sectors, and geographies can lead to higher costs and fees, including transaction fees, management fees, and taxes. Be mindful of these costs and consider using low-cost index funds or ETFs to achieve diversification at a lower cost.

3. Correlation:

While diversification aims to reduce risk by spreading investments across uncorrelated assets, some assets may still move in tandem during extreme market conditions. For example, during a financial crisis, both stocks and bonds may decline simultaneously. It's important to be aware of the correlation between assets in your portfolio and adjust your strategy as needed.

Conclusion: Building a Portfolio for the Long Term

Diversification is a key component of a successful investment strategy for the Minimalistic Entrepreneur. By spreading your investments across different asset classes, sectors, and geographies, you can reduce risk, enhance stability, and increase your chances of achieving long-term financial goals.

Building a diversified portfolio requires careful planning, regular monitoring, and disciplined rebalancing. It's about finding the right balance between risk and return, and creating a portfolio that aligns with your unique financial situation and investment objectives.

Remember, diversification is not a one-time event but an ongoing process. As you grow and evolve as an investor, your portfolio should adapt to reflect your changing goals and circumstances. By staying committed to the principles of diversification, you're setting yourself up for success in the stock market and paving the way for lasting financial freedom.

CHAPTER SIX

DIVERSIFICATION FOR THE MINIMALISTIC ENTREPRENEUR

In the ever-evolving landscape of investing, one principle stands as a timeless pillar of wisdom: diversification. It's a strategy that's often preached but not always fully understood. For the minimalistic entrepreneur, diversification isn't about owning a little bit of everything; it's about creating a portfolio that is as resilient as it is streamlined. This chapter delves into how diversification across multiple asset classes can be your most powerful tool in building wealth while adhering to the minimalist ethos.

At its core, diversification is about spreading risk without spreading yourself thin. It's about finding that sweet spot where your investments are secure yet poised for growth, where your portfolio is simple yet robust. By diversifying wisely, you align your financial strategy with the principles of minimalism—focusing on what truly matters, eliminating the unnecessary, and maintaining clarity in your investment decisions.

Why Diversification Matters:

In the world of investing, risk is an unavoidable companion. Markets rise and fall, industries thrive and falter, and global events can send shockwaves through even the most carefully curated portfolios. Diversification is your buffer against these uncertainties. By allocating your investments across a variety of asset classes, you reduce the impact of any single asset's poor performance on your overall portfolio. In essence, diversification allows you to safeguard your wealth while positioning yourself to seize opportunities for growth.

For the minimalistic entrepreneur, the goal is not just to survive market turbulence but to thrive within it. Diversification enables you to do just that by ensuring that your portfolio isn't overly dependent on any one asset or market. It's about creating a balanced approach that aligns with your long-term financial goals and risk tolerance.

Section 1: Understanding Asset Classes

What Are Asset Classes?

Before diving into the mechanics of diversification, it's crucial to understand what asset classes are and why they play such a vital role in your investment strategy. An asset class is essentially a group of securities that share similar characteristics, behave similarly in the marketplace, and are subject to the same laws and regulations. Each asset class offers distinct risk and return profiles, making them integral components of a well-rounded portfolio.

The concept of asset classes is foundational to diversification. By spreading your investments across different types of assets, you mitigate risk and enhance your portfolio's ability to weather various market conditions. But remember, as a minimalistic entrepreneur, the goal isn't to own a little bit of everything—it's to own a carefully selected mix of assets that align with your financial objectives.

Types of Asset Classes:

- Equities (Stocks):

Equities, or stocks, represent ownership in a company. When you purchase shares of a company, you're buying a stake in its future profits (or losses). Equities are known for their potential to deliver high returns, but with that potential comes increased risk. Stock prices can be volatile, influenced by factors ranging from company performance to broader economic trends.

For the minimalistic entrepreneur, the key to investing in equities is to focus on high-quality companies with strong fundamentals—businesses that align with your investment philosophy and long-term goals.

- Bonds (Fixed Income):

Bonds are essentially loans that you, as an investor, make to corporations or governments. In return, you receive regular interest payments over a specified period, with the principal amount returned at maturity. Bonds are generally considered safer than stocks, providing a steady income stream with lower risk. However, they also offer lower returns compared to equities. In a diversified portfolio, bonds serve as a stabilizing force, balancing the higher volatility of stocks and providing a reliable source of income.

- Real Estate:

Real estate investments involve purchasing property with the expectation of generating income or appreciation over time. This asset class includes residential, commercial, and industrial properties, each with its own risk and return characteristics. Real estate offers a tangible, physical asset that can act as a hedge against inflation and provide consistent rental income. For the minimalistic entrepreneur, real estate can be an attractive addition to a diversified portfolio, offering stability and potential growth in a sector that often moves independently of the stock market.

- Commodities:

Commodities are physical goods such as gold, silver, oil, and agricultural products. These assets can provide a hedge against inflation and currency fluctuations, as their prices often move inversely to traditional financial markets. Investing in commodities adds a layer of diversification that protects your portfolio from economic downturns and market volatility. However, commodities can be highly speculative, so it's essential to approach them with caution, selecting only those that align with your overall investment strategy.

- Alternative Investments:

Alternative investments encompass a wide range of assets that don't fall into the traditional categories of stocks, bonds, or cash. This includes private equity, hedge funds, venture capital, and even cryptocurrencies. These investments often offer higher potential returns but come with increased risk and lower liquidity. For the minimalistic entrepreneur, alternative investments can be a valuable addition to a diversified portfolio—provided they are chosen with care and a clear understanding of their role within your broader investment strategy.

Section 2: The Minimalistic Approach to Diversification

Strategic Simplicity:

In the realm of investing, diversification is often misunderstood as the practice of accumulating a vast array of assets. However, for the minimalistic entrepreneur, true diversification is about strategic simplicity—selecting a well-balanced mix of asset classes that complement each other and align with your specific financial goals. The aim is not to own everything but to own the right things.

Strategic simplicity means focusing on quality over quantity. It's about identifying the core assets that will drive your portfolio's performance and ensuring that each asset plays a distinct and complementary role. This approach not only simplifies your investment process but also enhances your ability to monitor and manage your portfolio effectively. By keeping your portfolio streamlined, you can maintain clarity and control, avoiding the pitfalls of over-diversification, where complexity can dilute returns and increase the risk of underperformance.

The Power of Balance:

At the heart of diversification is the concept of balance—balancing risk with reward, growth with stability, and short-term gains with long-term objectives. A diversified portfolio is like a well-composed symphony, where each instrument (or asset class) plays its part in harmony with the others. When one section falters, another can carry the tune, ensuring that the overall performance remains strong and consistent.

For the minimalistic entrepreneur, achieving this balance requires a thoughtful approach to asset allocation. It's about understanding how different asset classes interact and how their performance correlates—or doesn't—with one another. By carefully selecting a mix of assets that complement each other, you create a portfolio that is resilient to market fluctuations and positioned for steady growth over time.

Section 3: Building a Diversified Portfolio

Starting with Your Core:

The foundation of any diversified portfolio begins with the core asset classes—typically equities and bonds. These assets form the bedrock of your investment strategy, providing the growth potential and stability needed to achieve your financial goals. For the minimalistic entrepreneur, the key is to focus on high-quality, reliable investments that you can confidently hold over the long term.

When building your core, consider your risk tolerance, time horizon, and financial objectives. A younger investor with a longer time horizon might lean more heavily into equities, seeking higher returns through growth stocks. On the other hand, an investor nearing retirement may prioritize bonds for their income stability and lower risk profile. The goal is to strike a balance that aligns with your personal financial situation and long-term aspirations.

Adding Real Estate and Commodities:

Once your core is established, you can begin to diversify further by adding real estate and commodities to your portfolio. Real estate provides a tangible asset that often appreciates over time and can generate rental income, adding both stability and income potential. Commodities, such as gold or oil, offer protection against inflation and economic uncertainty, acting as a counterbalance to the volatility of stocks and bonds.

When incorporating these assets, it's essential to consider their unique characteristics and how they fit into your overall strategy. For example, real estate may require more hands-on management and carries liquidity risks, while commodities can be highly speculative and influenced by global events. As always, the minimalistic approach emphasizes quality over quantity—focus on a few well-chosen assets that complement your core holdings and contribute to a well-rounded, resilient portfolio.

Exploring Alternative Investments:

For those looking to diversify beyond traditional asset classes, alternative investments offer additional avenues for growth and risk management. These assets, which include private equity, hedge funds, and even cryptocurrencies, can provide significant returns and help diversify risk. However, they also come with higher volatility and lower liquidity, making them suitable only for those who have a solid core portfolio and are comfortable with the added complexity.

When exploring alternative investments, it's crucial to approach them with a clear understanding of their risks and rewards. These assets should be seen as supplements to your core portfolio, not replacements. The goal is to enhance diversification and potentially boost returns, while still adhering to the principles of minimalistic entrepreneurship—keeping your portfolio focused, manageable, and aligned with your long-term goals.

Section 4: Rebalancing for Long-Term Success

Why Rebalancing Matters:

Diversification is not a set-it-and-forget-it strategy. Over time, the performance of different asset classes will cause your portfolio to drift from its original allocation, potentially increasing your exposure to risk. Rebalancing is the process of realigning your portfolio to maintain your desired asset allocation, ensuring that your investment strategy remains consistent with your financial goals.

For the minimalistic entrepreneur, rebalancing is an essential practice that keeps your portfolio focused and aligned with your long-term objectives. It's a way to stay disciplined, avoiding the temptation to chase short-term gains or react impulsively to market fluctuations. By regularly rebalancing, you ensure that your portfolio remains diversified and balanced, reducing risk and enhancing the potential for steady, long-term growth.

When and How to Rebalance:

Rebalancing can be done on a regular schedule—such as annually or semi-annually—or in response to significant market movements. The key is to establish a rebalancing strategy that aligns with your investment philosophy and stick to it, even when the markets are volatile.

When rebalancing, consider the following steps:

- Assess your current allocation: Review your portfolio to determine how your assets have shifted from their original allocation.

- Determine your target allocation: Decide on the allocation that best fits your current financial goals and risk tolerance.

- Execute rebalancing: Sell and buy assets as needed to realign your portfolio with your target allocation. Consider transaction costs and tax implications when making these adjustments.

- Stay disciplined: Rebalancing may require selling high-performing assets and buying those that have underperformed, which can be emotionally challenging. Trust the process and remain committed to your long-term strategy.

By rebalancing regularly, you maintain control over your portfolio, ensuring that it continues to reflect your minimalist approach to investing—focused, intentional, and aligned with your long-term goals.

Section 5: The Minimalist's Guide to Global Diversification

Going Global:

In today's interconnected world, diversification isn't just about spreading your investments across different asset classes—it's also about considering the benefits of global diversification. By including international assets in your portfolio, you gain exposure to different economies, industries, and markets, reducing your reliance on any single region and enhancing your portfolio's resilience.

For the minimalistic entrepreneur, global diversification offers a way to expand your horizons while maintaining a focused, efficient investment strategy. It allows you to capitalize on growth opportunities in emerging markets, hedge against domestic market risks, and gain access to industries that may not be well-represented in your home country.

Simplifying Global Investments:

While global diversification offers many benefits, it can also introduce complexity. Different currencies, regulations, and economic conditions can make international investing challenging. However, a minimalist approach to global diversification focuses on simplicity—using tools and investment vehicles that make global investing accessible and manageable.

Consider the following strategies for global diversification:

- Global ETFs and Mutual Funds: These investment vehicles provide exposure to international markets without the need to manage individual foreign stocks or bonds.

- Currency Hedging: Protect your portfolio from currency risk by using hedged investment options or implementing currency-hedging strategies.

- Focus on Key Markets: Rather than investing in every market, consider focusing on regions or countries with strong growth potential and economic stability.

By incorporating global assets into your portfolio thoughtfully and strategically, you enhance diversification while maintaining the clarity and simplicity that define the minimalistic approach to investing.

Conclusion: Diversification as a Pillar of Minimalistic Entrepreneurship

Summing Up the Power of Diversification:

Diversification across multiple asset classes is more than just a risk management strategy—it's a core principle of minimalistic entrepreneurship. By carefully selecting and balancing your investments, you create a portfolio that is not only resilient but also aligned with your financial goals. This approach allows you to minimize risk, maximize returns, and maintain focus on what truly matters.

Action Steps for the Reader:

As you reflect on the principles of diversification, take the time to evaluate your current portfolio. Consider how you can incorporate the strategies discussed in this chapter to enhance your diversification, simplify your investments, and align your portfolio with your long-term goals. Use the checklist below to guide your next steps:

- Review your current asset allocation: Are you adequately diversified across multiple asset classes?

- Identify gaps in your portfolio: Are there opportunities to add new asset classes or reduce overexposure to any single investment?

- Create a rebalancing plan: Establish a schedule and strategy for rebalancing your portfolio to maintain your desired allocation.

- Consider global diversification: Explore opportunities to include international assets in your portfolio.

By taking these steps, you'll strengthen your investment strategy, embracing the minimalist approach to diversification and securing your path to long-term financial success.

CHAPTER SEVEN

Risk Management and Long-Term Thinking

Understanding and Mitigating Investment Risks

Investing in the stock market offers the potential for significant returns, but it also comes with inherent risks. As a Minimalistic Entrepreneur, understanding and managing these risks is crucial to achieving your financial goals and protecting your hard-earned capital. Risk management is not about avoiding risk altogether—because that's impossible—but about making informed decisions that minimize the impact of potential losses while allowing you to take advantage of growth opportunities.

In this chapter, we'll explore the different types of investment risks you might encounter, techniques to assess these risks, and strategies to mitigate them effectively. By the end of this chapter, you'll be equipped with the knowledge and tools to manage your investments with confidence, ensuring that your portfolio is resilient enough to withstand market fluctuations and unforeseen challenges.

Types of Investment Risks

Investment risks come in various forms, each with its own potential impact on your portfolio. Understanding these risks is the first step toward managing them effectively. Let's delve into the most common types of investment risks that every investor should be aware of:

1. Market Risk:

Market risk, also known as systematic risk, refers to the risk of losing money due to changes in the overall market. This type of risk affects all investments, regardless of the specific stock or asset class. Market risk is driven by factors such as economic recessions, political instability, changes in interest rates, and global events.

- Equity Risk: Equity risk is the risk of losing money due to a decline in stock prices. Stock prices can fluctuate based on company performance, industry trends, and broader market conditions. Even the best-performing companies can experience stock price declines during market downturns.

- Interest Rate Risk: Interest rate risk is the risk that changes in interest rates will negatively impact the value of your investments, particularly bonds. When interest rates rise, bond prices typically fall, and vice versa. This is because new bonds are issued with higher interest rates, making existing bonds with lower rates less attractive.

- Currency Risk: Currency risk, or exchange rate risk, occurs when you invest in foreign assets. Fluctuations in currency exchange rates can affect the value of your investments. For example, if the Indian rupee depreciates against the U.S. dollar, the value of your U.S. dollar-denominated investments may increase when converted back to rupees.

- Inflation Risk: Inflation risk is the risk that the purchasing power of your investments will be eroded by rising prices. Inflation reduces the real value of your returns, especially if your investments do not outpace inflation over time.

2. Specific Risk:

Specific risk, also known as unsystematic risk, is the risk associated with a particular company or industry. Unlike market risk, specific risk can be mitigated through diversification.

- Business Risk: Business risk refers to the risk that a company's performance will decline due to internal factors such as poor management, product failures, or changes in consumer preferences. For example, if a company's new product launch fails to meet expectations, its stock price may decline.

- Financial Risk: Financial risk is related to a company's use of debt. Companies with high levels of debt are more vulnerable to financial distress, especially during economic downturns. If a company is unable to meet its debt obligations, it may face bankruptcy, leading to a loss of value for shareholders.

- Operational Risk: Operational risk arises from the day-to-day operations of a company. This includes risks related to supply chain disruptions, technological failures, regulatory compliance, and human error. For example, a major data breach can damage a company's reputation and lead to financial losses.

- Legal and Regulatory Risk: Legal and regulatory risk involves the potential for losses due to changes in laws, regulations, or legal actions. Companies operating in heavily regulated industries, such as pharmaceuticals or finance, are particularly exposed to this type of risk.

3. Liquidity Risk:

Liquidity risk is the risk that you won't be able to sell an investment quickly without affecting its price. This risk is particularly relevant for investments in small-cap stocks, real estate, or other assets that are not traded frequently. If you need to sell an illiquid asset quickly, you may have to accept a lower price than you would in a more liquid market.

4. Credit Risk:

Credit risk, or default risk, is the risk that a borrower will be unable to meet its debt obligations. This risk is most relevant for bond investors, as it affects the likelihood that you will receive the interest payments and principal repayment you are owed. Credit risk is higher for bonds issued by companies with lower credit ratings or by governments with unstable economies.

5. Reinvestment Risk:

Reinvestment risk is the risk that you will have to reinvest the proceeds from a maturing investment at a lower interest rate than the original investment. This risk is particularly relevant for bond investors. For example, if interest rates decline, the income you earn from reinvesting in new bonds may be lower than the income from the original bonds.

6. Concentration Risk:

Concentration risk occurs when your portfolio is heavily weighted toward a particular asset, sector, or geographic region. This lack of diversification increases the potential for significant losses if that specific area underperforms. For example, if your portfolio is heavily concentrated in technology stocks, a downturn in the tech sector could lead to substantial losses.

Risk Assessment Techniques

Once you understand the types of risks you may face, the next step is to assess the level of risk in your portfolio. Risk assessment techniques help you identify potential vulnerabilities in your investments and make informed decisions about how to manage them.

1. Standard Deviation:

Standard deviation is a statistical measure that quantifies the volatility of an investment's returns. A higher standard deviation indicates greater volatility, meaning the investment's returns are more likely to fluctuate widely. By calculating the standard deviation of your portfolio, you can gauge the level of risk associated with your investments.

- Application: Use standard deviation to compare the risk levels of different investments or portfolios. For example, if two stocks have similar expected returns, the one with the lower standard deviation is considered less risky.

2. Beta:

Beta is a measure of a stock's volatility relative to the overall market. A beta of 1 indicates that the stock's price tends to move in line with the market. A beta greater than 1 indicates higher volatility than the market, while a beta less than 1 indicates lower volatility.

- Application: Use beta to assess the risk of individual stocks within your portfolio. If you prefer a lower-risk portfolio, focus on stocks with lower betas. Conversely, if you're willing to take on more risk for higher potential returns, you may consider stocks with higher betas.

3. Value at Risk (VaR):

Value at Risk (VaR) is a statistical technique that estimates the maximum potential loss of an investment over a specified period, given a certain level of confidence. VaR helps you understand the potential downside of your investments in the worst-case scenario.

- Application: Use VaR to assess the potential losses in your portfolio over a specific time frame, such as a day, week, or month. This technique is particularly useful for risk management in volatile markets.

4. Stress Testing:

Stress testing involves simulating extreme market conditions to assess how your portfolio would perform under adverse scenarios. This technique helps identify vulnerabilities in your portfolio that may not be apparent during normal market conditions.

- Application: Use stress testing to evaluate the impact of events such as a market crash, interest rate hike, or economic recession on your portfolio. This can help you prepare for potential market shocks and make adjustments to your portfolio as needed.

5. Scenario Analysis:

Scenario analysis is similar to stress testing but involves considering multiple hypothetical scenarios that could impact your portfolio. These scenarios may include both positive and negative outcomes, allowing you to assess the potential range of returns for your investments.

- Application: Use scenario analysis to explore different market conditions and their potential impact on your portfolio. For example, you might consider how your portfolio would perform in a high-growth scenario versus a recessionary scenario.

Strategies to Minimize Risk

While it's impossible to eliminate all investment risks, there are several strategies you can use to minimize their impact on your portfolio. These strategies are designed to help you manage risk effectively while still pursuing your financial goals.

1. Diversification:

Diversification is the practice of spreading your investments across different asset classes, sectors, and geographic regions to reduce the impact of any single investment's poor performance. By diversifying your portfolio, you can mitigate specific risks and enhance the stability of your overall returns.

- Application: Create a diversified portfolio that includes a mix of stocks, bonds, real estate, and cash. Within each asset class, diversify further by investing in different sectors, industries, and geographic regions.

2. Asset Allocation:

Asset allocation involves determining the optimal mix of asset classes in your portfolio based on your risk tolerance, financial goals, and time horizon. By balancing your investments across different asset classes, you can manage risk and improve the potential for long-term returns.

- Application: Regularly review and adjust your asset allocation to ensure it remains aligned with your goals and risk tolerance. For example, if you're nearing retirement, you may want to shift your allocation toward more conservative investments, such as bonds and cash.

3. Rebalancing:

Rebalancing is the process of adjusting your portfolio's asset allocation to maintain your desired level of risk. Over time, the value of your investments may fluctuate, causing your portfolio to drift from its original allocation. Rebalancing helps bring your portfolio back in line with your target allocation.

- Application: Set a regular schedule for rebalancing your portfolio, such as annually or semi-annually. During rebalancing, sell some of your overperforming assets and reinvest the proceeds in underperforming assets to restore your desired allocation.

4. Hedging:

Hedging is a strategy used to offset potential losses in one investment by taking an opposite position in another investment. Hedging can help protect your portfolio from adverse market movements, though it may also limit potential gains.

- Application: Consider using derivatives, such as options or futures, to hedge against specific risks in your portfolio. For example, if you hold a significant position in a stock, you might use options to hedge against potential price declines.

5. Using Stop-Loss Orders:

A stop-loss order is an automatic order to sell a security when it reaches a certain price, helping to limit potential losses. Stop-loss orders can be an effective way to protect your portfolio from significant declines without requiring constant monitoring.

- Application: Set stop-loss orders on individual stocks or other investments to automatically sell if the price falls below a predetermined level. This can help you limit losses during market downturns while allowing you to stay invested for potential rebounds.

6. Staggering Maturities:

If you invest in bonds or other fixed-income securities, staggering maturities (also known as laddering) is a strategy that involves holding bonds with different maturity dates. This approach helps reduce reinvestment risk and interest rate risk by spreading out the maturities of your investments.

- Application: Build a bond ladder by purchasing bonds with varying maturities, such as 1-year, 5-year, and 10-year bonds. As each bond matures, reinvest the proceeds in new bonds with similar maturities to maintain the ladder.

7. Investing in High-Quality Assets:

Investing in high-quality assets, such as blue-chip stocks, investment-grade bonds, and well-established real estate, can help reduce risk. High-quality assets are generally more stable and less likely to experience significant declines during market downturns.

- Application: Focus on investing in companies with strong financials, a history of consistent earnings, and a competitive advantage. Similarly, choose bonds with high credit ratings and properties in desirable locations to enhance the quality of your portfolio.

8. Long-Term Perspective:

Maintaining a long-term perspective is one of the most effective ways to manage risk. While short-term market fluctuations can be unsettling, staying focused on your long-term goals can help you avoid making impulsive decisions based on temporary market movements.

- Application: Keep your investment horizon in mind and resist the urge to react to short-term market volatility. Remember that the stock market has historically trended upward over the long term, and staying invested through market cycles can lead to significant wealth accumulation.

Conclusion: Embracing Risk as Part of the Journey

Risk is an inherent part of investing, but it doesn't have to be something to fear. By understanding the types of risks you may face and employing effective risk management strategies, you can navigate the stock market with confidence and resilience. As a Minimalistic Entrepreneur, your goal is to build a portfolio that not only aligns with your financial goals but also stands the test of time, regardless of market conditions.

Remember, successful investing is not about avoiding risk altogether but about managing it wisely. By diversifying your portfolio, assessing risks regularly, and employing strategies to mitigate potential losses, you can protect your investments and continue to grow your wealth over the long term. Embrace risk as part of the journey, and use the tools and techniques outlined in this chapter to make informed, strategic decisions that will guide you toward financial freedom.

The Power of Compound Interest

If there's one concept that every Minimalistic Entrepreneur should fully grasp and appreciate, it's the power of compound interest. Often referred to as the "eighth wonder of the world" by Albert Einstein, compound interest is the engine behind wealth accumulation. It's the process by which your investments grow exponentially over time, as the returns you earn begin to generate their own returns. Understanding and leveraging the power of compound interest is key to achieving financial freedom and building lasting wealth.

In this Part, we'll dive deep into the concept of compound interest, explore its long-term impact on your wealth, and discuss practical tools like calculators and projections that can help you visualize its effects on your financial future. By the end of this chapter, you'll have a clear understanding of how to harness the power of compound interest to supercharge your investment strategy.

Explanation of Compound Interest: The Magic of Growth

At its core, compound interest is the process of earning interest on both your original investment (the principal) and the interest that has already been added to that investment. Unlike simple interest, which is calculated only on the principal, compound interest allows your wealth to grow at an accelerating rate because the interest itself begins to earn interest.

How Compound Interest Works

Let's break down how compound interest works with a simple example:
Imagine you invest ₹1,00,000 at an annual interest rate of 10%. With simple interest, you would earn ₹10,000 every year, resulting in a total of ₹1,50,000 after five years.

However, with compound interest, your interest is added to your principal each year, so you earn interest not just on the original ₹ 1,00,000, but also on the interest that has been added over time:
- Year 1: ₹1,00,000 + 10% = ₹1,10,000
- Year 2: ₹1,10,000 + 10% = ₹1,21,000
- Year 3: ₹1,21,000 + 10% = ₹1,33,100

- Year 4:   ₹1,33,100 + 10% =   ₹1,46,410
- Year 5:   ₹1,46,410 + 10% =   ₹1,61,051

After five years, your investment has grown to   ₹1,61,051, compared to   ₹1,50,000 with simple interest. While this difference may seem small at first, it becomes increasingly significant over time, especially with larger investments and longer periods.

Compounding Frequency

One important factor in the power of compound interest is the frequency of compounding. Compounding can occur on different schedules—annually, semi-annually, quarterly, monthly, or even daily. The more frequently interest is compounded, the faster your investment will grow.

For example, if the   ₹1,00,000 investment mentioned earlier is compounded quarterly instead of annually at the same 10% rate, the investment would grow even more quickly:

- Year 1:   ₹1,00,000 compounded quarterly at 10% =   ₹1,10,381
- Year 5:   ₹1,00,000 compounded quarterly at 10% =   ₹1,63,863

As you can see, more frequent compounding leads to higher returns, highlighting the importance of choosing investment vehicles that offer frequent compounding.

Long-Term Impact on Wealth Building

The true power of compound interest reveals itself over the long term. The longer your money is invested and allowed to compound, the greater the growth. This exponential growth can have a transformative impact on your financial future, turning even modest investments into substantial wealth over time.

The Rule of 72

One simple way to estimate how long it will take for your investment to double with compound interest is by using the Rule of 72. This rule states that you can divide 72 by your annual interest rate to determine the number of years it will take for your investment to double.

For example, with an annual interest rate of 10%, it will take approximately 7.2 years for your investment to double (72 ÷ 10 = 7.2 years). This rule provides a quick and easy way to understand the impact of compound interest on your investment growth.

Time is Your Greatest Ally

When it comes to compound interest, time is your greatest ally. The earlier you start investing, the more time your money has to compound, and the greater your wealth will grow. This is why it's so important to start investing as early as possible, even if you can only contribute a small amount initially.

Consider two investors: one starts investing ₹10,000 per year at age 25 and stops at age 35, while the other starts investing ₹10,000 per year at age 35 and continues until age 65. Assuming an annual return of 8%, the first investor's investment grows significantly more, even though they contributed for only 10 years, because of the power of compounding over a longer period.

- Investor 1 (starts at age 25):
- Total contribution: ₹1,00,000
- Value at age 65: ₹15,87,600
- Investor 2 (starts at age 35):
- Total contribution: ₹3,00,000
- Value at age 65: ₹12,27,300

Despite contributing less, the first investor ends up with more wealth, thanks to the longer compounding period. This example illustrates the importance of starting early and letting compound interest work its magic over time.

Harnessing Compound Interest in Your Investment Strategy

To make the most of compound interest, it's essential to incorporate it into your overall investment strategy. Here's how you can harness the power of compounding to build wealth effectively:

1. Start Early and Invest Regularly:

The earlier you start investing, the more time your money has to compound. Even small, regular contributions can grow into substantial sums over time. Make it a habit to invest a portion of your income regularly, whether it's through systematic investment plans (SIPs), retirement accounts, or direct investments in the stock market.

2. Reinvest Your Earnings:

To maximize the benefits of compound interest, reinvest your earnings, including dividends and interest payments. Reinvesting allows your returns to compound over time, leading to even greater growth. Many investment platforms offer automatic dividend reinvestment plans (DRIPs), making it easy to reinvest your earnings without additional effort.

3. Choose Investments with Frequent Compounding:

When selecting investment vehicles, consider those that offer frequent compounding, such as savings accounts with daily interest calculations, mutual funds that reinvest dividends, or stocks that pay regular dividends. The more frequently your investment compounds, the faster it will grow.

4. Stay Invested for the Long Term:

The true power of compound interest is unlocked over the long term. While market fluctuations and economic cycles can cause short-term volatility, staying invested allows your money to compound uninterrupted. Avoid the temptation to withdraw your investments prematurely, and focus on your long-term financial goals.

5. Take Advantage of Tax-Deferred Accounts:

Tax-deferred accounts, such as retirement accounts (e.g., PPF, EPF, NPS), allow your investments to grow tax-free until you withdraw them. This tax advantage enhances the power of compound interest by allowing more of your returns to be reinvested and compounded over time.

Calculators and Projections: Visualizing the Power of Compounding

One of the most effective ways to appreciate the power of compound interest is to see it in action through calculators and projections. These tools allow you to input different variables, such as the initial investment amount, interest rate, compounding frequency, and investment duration, to visualize how your money will grow over time.

Using Compound Interest Calculators

Compound interest calculators are widely available online and are simple to use. By entering a few key details, you can generate projections of how your investments will grow. Here's how to use these calculators effectively:

1. Initial Investment: Enter the amount of money you plan to invest initially. This could be a lump sum or the total of your first year's contributions.

2. Regular Contributions: Specify how much you plan to contribute regularly, whether it's monthly, quarterly, or annually. Regular contributions significantly boost the power of compounding.

3. Interest Rate: Input the expected annual interest rate or return on your investment. Be realistic in your assumptions, considering the historical performance of your chosen investment type.

4. Compounding Frequency: Select the compounding frequency (e.g., annually, semi-annually, quarterly, monthly). As mentioned earlier, more frequent compounding leads to faster growth.

5. Investment Duration: Specify how long you plan to keep the investment. The longer the duration, the greater the impact of compound interest.

6. Calculate and Project: Once you've entered all the details, calculate the results to see how your investment will grow over time. Most calculators will provide a projection graph, showing the exponential growth of your investment as compound interest takes effect.

Understanding Projections

Projections generated by compound interest calculators can be incredibly motivating. They show how small, consistent contributions can grow into substantial sums over time. However, it's important to remember that these projections are based on assumptions and are not guarantees of future performance. Market conditions, economic factors, and changes in interest rates can all impact your actual returns.

Use projections as a tool to guide your investment decisions, but remain flexible and adaptable as you progress on your financial journey. Regularly review and update your projections to reflect changes in your financial situation, investment goals, and market conditions.

Conclusion: Let Compound Interest Be Your Wealth-Building Partner

Let compound interest be your silent partner in building wealth. It's a force that works quietly in the background, steadily growing your investments over time. As a Minimalistic Entrepreneur, understanding and harnessing the power of compound interest is one of the most effective strategies for achieving financial freedom.

The key to maximizing the benefits of compound interest is consistency and patience. Start investing early, contribute regularly, and stay committed to your long-term goals. The sooner you begin, the more time you give your investments to grow exponentially. Remember, even modest amounts can turn into substantial sums over time when compounded.

However, it's important to recognize that while compound interest is powerful, it's not a magic bullet. It requires a disciplined approach, careful planning, and a commitment to your investment strategy. Regularly monitor your investments, make adjustments as needed, and stay informed about market trends and economic conditions. By doing so, you'll ensure that your money continues to work for you, compounding and growing as you move closer to your financial goals.

Finally, never underestimate the impact of compound interest on your financial journey. It's not just about the numbers; it's about the peace of mind that comes from knowing you're building a secure and prosperous future. By embracing the power of compound interest, you're taking a crucial step toward realizing your dreams and achieving the financial freedom that comes with a well-managed, growing portfolio.

Let compound interest work its magic, and over time, you'll see the rewards in the form of a robust and resilient financial foundation—one that will support your aspirations and provide the freedom to live life on your terms.

Patience and Emotional Control in Investing

The stock market is a dynamic environment, subject to fluctuations that can test even the most seasoned investor. Market volatility, sudden downturns, and unexpected news can trigger emotional responses that, if not managed, may lead to impulsive decisions detrimental to your financial goals. As a Minimalistic Entrepreneur, mastering patience and emotional control is not just advisable—it's essential. These qualities are the bedrock of a disciplined investment strategy that can withstand the inevitable ups and downs of the market.

In this part, we will explore how to deal with market volatility, avoid common emotional pitfalls, and develop a disciplined approach to investing. By the end of this chapter, you'll be equipped with the mindset and strategies needed to navigate the psychological challenges of investing, helping you stay the course toward your long-term financial objectives.

Dealing with Market Volatility: Staying Calm in the Storm

Market volatility refers to the rapid and unpredictable changes in stock prices that can occur over short periods. Volatility is a natural part of the stock market, driven by factors such as economic data releases, political events, changes in interest rates, and shifts in investor sentiment. While volatility can create opportunities for profit, it can also lead to anxiety and panic if not properly managed.

Understanding the Nature of Volatility

To effectively deal with market volatility, it's important to understand that it is not inherently negative. Volatility is a reflection of the market's constant re-evaluation of asset prices based on new information. It's the market's way of adjusting to changes in economic conditions, corporate earnings, and global events.

For the Minimalistic Entrepreneur, recognizing that volatility is a normal part of the investment landscape can help reduce the emotional impact of short-term price movements. Instead of fearing volatility, learn to view it as an opportunity to assess and, if appropriate, adjust your portfolio.

Strategies for Managing Volatility

1. Focus on the Long Term:

One of the most effective ways to manage the emotional impact of volatility is to maintain a long-term perspective. Remember that the stock market has historically trended upward over the long run, despite periods of volatility and downturns.

   - Application: When market volatility strikes, revisit your long-term financial goals and remind yourself why you invested in the first place. Avoid making decisions based on short-term price movements, and instead focus on the fundamental strength of your investments.

2. Stay Informed, Not Obsessed:

It's important to stay informed about the market and your investments, but there's a fine line between being informed and being obsessed. Constantly checking stock prices or reacting to every piece of news can lead to stress and impulsive decisions.

   - Application: Set specific times to review your portfolio and market news, rather than constantly monitoring them throughout the day. Trust in your research and investment strategy, and avoid the temptation to react to every market fluctuation.

3. Diversify Your Portfolio:

As discussed in earlier chapters, diversification is a key strategy for managing risk, including the risk associated with volatility. A well-diversified portfolio can help cushion the impact of market downturns by spreading risk across different asset classes, sectors, and geographies.

   - Application: Ensure that your portfolio is diversified to reduce the impact of volatility on any single investment. If one sector or asset class experiences a downturn, the losses may be offset by gains in other areas of your portfolio.

4. Use Dollar-Cost Averaging:

Dollar-cost averaging (DCA) is a strategy where you invest a fixed amount of money at regular intervals, regardless of the market's performance. This approach reduces the emotional impact of volatility by spreading your investments over time, allowing you to buy more shares when prices are low and fewer shares when prices are high.

- Application: Implement DCA by setting up automatic contributions to your investment accounts, such as a systematic investment plan (SIP). This strategy helps you stay committed to investing consistently, even during periods of market volatility.

Avoiding Common Emotional Pitfalls: The Traps to Watch Out For Emotions are a natural part of the human experience, but they can be detrimental when it comes to investing. Fear, greed, impatience, and overconfidence are just a few of the emotions that can lead to poor investment decisions. By recognizing and avoiding these common emotional pitfalls, you can stay focused on your long-term goals and avoid costly mistakes.

Fear and Panic

Fear is one of the most powerful emotions in investing. It often arises during market downturns, when the value of your investments declines, and uncertainty prevails. Fear can lead to panic selling, where investors liquidate their holdings at a loss, driven by the fear of further declines.

- Avoiding the Trap: The key to overcoming fear is to maintain perspective. Market downturns are a normal part of the investment cycle, and history shows that markets tend to recover over time. Instead of reacting to fear, focus on the fundamentals of your investments and remember that short-term losses are not realized until you sell.

Greed and Overconfidence

Greed can be just as dangerous as fear. It often manifests during bull markets, when asset prices are rising, and investors become overly optimistic. Greed can lead to chasing after high returns, taking on excessive risk, or holding on to investments for too long in the hope of even higher gains.

- Avoiding the Trap: To counteract greed, set realistic expectations and establish clear investment criteria. Avoid the temptation to chase after "hot" stocks or sectors without proper research. Remember that investing is a marathon, not a sprint, and that slow and steady growth is often more sustainable than rapid gains.

Impatience

Impatience is another common emotional pitfall, especially in today's fast-paced world. The desire for quick results can lead to frequent trading, abandoning long-term strategies, or reacting to short-term market movements.

- Avoiding the Trap: Cultivate patience by committing to your long-term investment plan and resisting the urge to make frequent changes. Understand that wealth-building through investing takes time, and that compounding, as discussed in the previous chapter, is most effective over the long term.

Confirmation Bias

Confirmation bias occurs when investors seek out information that confirms their existing beliefs while ignoring or downplaying information that contradicts them. This bias can lead to poor decision-making and the reinforcement of flawed investment strategies.

- Avoiding the Trap: To combat confirmation bias, seek out diverse perspectives and be open to changing your views based on new information. Regularly review your investment thesis and be willing to adjust your strategy if the facts no longer support it.

Developing a Disciplined Approach: Building Mental Resilience

Discipline is the cornerstone of successful investing. It's what allows you to stick to your investment plan, avoid emotional decision-making, and stay focused on your long-term goals. Developing a disciplined approach requires mental resilience, a clear strategy, and a commitment to continuous learning.

Creating a Clear Investment Plan

A clear investment plan is the foundation of discipline. Your plan should outline your financial goals, risk tolerance, asset allocation, and investment criteria. It serves as a roadmap that guides your decisions and keeps you on track, even when emotions run high.

- Application: Develop a written investment plan that includes specific goals, such as retirement savings, purchasing a home, or funding education. Define your risk tolerance and determine the appropriate asset allocation for your portfolio. Establish criteria for selecting investments, such as minimum return requirements, maximum acceptable risk, and preferred investment vehicles.

Sticking to Your Strategy

Once you've established your investment plan, the next challenge is sticking to it. This means resisting the urge to deviate from your strategy based on short-term market movements or emotional impulses.

- Application: Review your investment plan regularly and remind yourself of your long-term goals. When faced with market volatility or external pressures, return to your plan and ask yourself whether any changes are truly warranted or if you're reacting emotionally. Make adjustments only when they align with your long-term objectives.

Continuous Learning and Adaptation

The investment landscape is constantly evolving, and successful investors are those who continuously learn and adapt. Staying informed about market trends, economic developments, and new investment opportunities can help you refine your strategy and maintain discipline.

- Application: Commit to ongoing education by reading financial news, attending investment seminars, and studying successful investors. Learn from both your successes and mistakes, and be willing to adapt your strategy as you gain more experience and knowledge.

Practicing Mindfulness

Mindfulness—the practice of being fully present and aware of your thoughts and emotions—can be a powerful tool for managing the psychological challenges of investing. By practicing mindfulness, you can develop greater self-awareness, reduce stress, and make more deliberate, thoughtful decisions.

- Application: Incorporate mindfulness techniques into your daily routine, such as meditation, deep breathing exercises, or simply taking a few moments to reflect before making investment decisions. Mindfulness can help you recognize emotional triggers and respond to them with greater clarity and composure.

Building Mental Resilience

Mental resilience is the ability to bounce back from setbacks and maintain a positive outlook, even in the face of challenges. In investing, resilience is essential for weathering market downturns, recovering from losses, and staying committed to your long-term goals.

- Application: Build resilience by cultivating a growth mindset—viewing challenges as opportunities to learn and grow. Surround yourself with supportive mentors, peers, and resources that reinforce your commitment to disciplined investing. Celebrate your progress and recognize that setbacks are a natural part of the journey.

Conclusion: Mastering Patience and Emotional Control

Patience and emotional control are the unsung heroes of successful investing. While market knowledge and analytical skills are important, it's your ability to manage emotions and stay disciplined that will ultimately determine your success as a Minimalistic Entrepreneur.

By developing a clear investment plan, practicing mindfulness, and building mental resilience, you can navigate the psychological challenges of investing with confidence. Remember, the stock market is a long-term game, and those who maintain patience and emotional control are best positioned to reap the rewards of their efforts.

Stay focused on your goals, trust in your strategy, and embrace the journey with calm and composure. With patience and emotional control, you'll not only achieve your financial objectives but also cultivate a mindset that will serve you well in all areas of life.

CHAPTER EIGHT

ADVANCED STOCK MARKET STRATEGIES

Dividend Investing

As you grow more comfortable with the stock market and begin to build a robust portfolio, you may start exploring advanced strategies that can further enhance your returns and provide steady income. One such strategy is dividend investing, a time-tested approach that involves investing in companies that pay regular dividends to their shareholders. Dividend investing not only offers the potential for capital appreciation but also provides a reliable stream of income, making it an attractive option for both conservative and growth-oriented investors.

In this chapter, we will delve into the benefits of dividend stocks, explore the concept of dividend growth investing, and discuss the risks and considerations that come with this strategy. By the end of this chapter, you'll have a comprehensive understanding of how to incorporate dividend investing into your portfolio, enabling you to build wealth while enjoying the security of regular income.

Benefits of Dividend Stocks: The Power of Passive Income

Dividend stocks are shares of companies that distribute a portion of their earnings to shareholders in the form of dividends, typically on a quarterly basis. These companies are often well-established, financially stable, and have a history of consistent profitability. Investing in dividend-paying stocks offers several key benefits, making it an appealing strategy for long-term investors.

Steady Income Stream

One of the most significant advantages of dividend stocks is the steady income they provide. Unlike growth stocks, which primarily offer the potential for capital appreciation, dividend stocks reward investors with regular cash payments. This income can be particularly valuable for retirees, those seeking to supplement their earnings, or anyone looking for a reliable source of passive income.

- Application: To maximize the benefits of dividend income, consider investing in a diversified portfolio of high-quality dividend-paying stocks across different sectors. This approach can help ensure a steady income stream, even if one or more companies reduce or suspend their dividends.

Compounding Returns Through Reinvestment

Another powerful benefit of dividend investing is the ability to reinvest dividends to compound your returns over time. When you reinvest your dividends, you purchase additional shares of the stock, which in turn generate more dividends in the future. This compounding effect can significantly enhance your overall returns, especially when done consistently over many years.

- Application: Take advantage of dividend reinvestment plans (DRIPs) offered by many brokerage firms. DRIPs allow you to automatically reinvest your dividends without incurring additional transaction fees, accelerating the compounding process and growing your investment more quickly.

Potential for Capital Appreciation

While dividend stocks are often associated with income, they can also provide capital appreciation. Many dividend-paying companies are well-established businesses with strong market positions, which allows them to grow over time. As these companies expand and increase their earnings, their stock prices may rise, providing you with both income and capital gains.

- Application: Look for dividend stocks with a history of earnings growth and a solid business model. Companies that consistently increase their dividends over time often have strong financials and a commitment to returning value to shareholders, making them attractive long-term investments.

Lower Volatility and Risk

Dividend-paying stocks tend to be less volatile than non-dividend-paying stocks, particularly during market downturns. This lower volatility is partly due to the fact that investors often view dividends as a sign of a company's financial health and stability. Additionally, the regular income from dividends can cushion the impact of falling stock prices, reducing the overall risk of your portfolio.

- Application: Incorporate dividend-paying stocks into your portfolio as a way to reduce overall volatility and provide a measure of stability. This is particularly important during periods of market uncertainty, when having a portion of your portfolio in reliable dividend stocks can help you weather the storm.

Tax Advantages

In many countries, including India, dividend income may be subject to preferential tax treatment compared to other forms of income, such as interest or wages. Depending on your tax bracket, this can make dividend investing a more tax-efficient strategy for generating income.

- Application: Be sure to understand the tax implications of dividend income in your country and consider the tax efficiency of your investments. Consult with a tax advisor if necessary to optimize your dividend strategy and minimize your tax liability.

Dividend Growth Investing: Building Wealth Over Time

Dividend growth investing is a strategy that focuses on companies with a history of consistently increasing their dividends over time. These companies, often referred to as "dividend growers," are typically financially strong, with stable earnings, a commitment to returning value to shareholders, and a track record of dividend increases. Dividend growth investing combines the benefits of regular income with the potential for long-term capital appreciation, making it an attractive strategy for wealth building.

Why Dividend Growth Matters

Dividend growth is a key indicator of a company's financial health and management's confidence in the future. Companies that consistently increase their dividends demonstrate that they are generating sufficient cash flow, managing their resources effectively, and are committed to rewarding shareholders. Over time, dividend growth can significantly enhance your income stream and overall returns.

Finding Dividend Growers

Identifying companies with strong dividend growth potential requires careful research and analysis. Here are some factors to consider when selecting dividend growth stocks:

1. Dividend History:

Look for companies with a long track record of dividend payments and increases. A history of consistent dividend growth, particularly over decades, is a strong indicator of a company's stability and financial strength. Companies that have increased their dividends through various economic cycles are often well-positioned to continue doing so in the future.

- Application: Focus on companies that have been paying and increasing dividends for at least 10-20 years. This track record suggests that the company has weathered economic downturns and remains committed to returning value to shareholders.

2. Payout Ratio:

The payout ratio is the percentage of a company's earnings that is paid out as dividends. A lower payout ratio suggests that the company has room to increase dividends in the future, while a very high payout ratio may indicate that the company is distributing too much of its earnings and may struggle to maintain or grow dividends during tough times.

- Application: Aim for companies with a payout ratio of 40% to 60%. This range typically indicates a healthy balance between paying dividends and retaining earnings for growth.

3. Earnings Growth:

Consistent earnings growth is essential for sustaining and increasing dividends. Companies that generate stable or growing earnings are more likely to continue raising their dividends over time. Focus on companies with a history of earnings growth and strong future growth prospects.

- Application: Look for companies with a solid earnings growth rate of 5% to 10% or higher. Strong earnings growth supports dividend increases and contributes to capital appreciation.

4. Strong Balance Sheet:

A company's financial strength is critical to its ability to maintain and grow dividends. Companies with low debt levels, strong cash flow, and a healthy balance sheet are better positioned to continue paying dividends even during challenging economic periods.

- Application: Prioritize companies with low debt-to-equity ratios and strong free cash flow. These financial indicators suggest that the company has the resources to support dividend payments and withstand economic downturns.

5. Dividend Yield:

While dividend yield is important, it should not be the sole factor in selecting dividend growth stocks. A high yield may be attractive, but it can also be a sign of potential risk, especially if the yield is significantly higher than the market average. Focus on a balance between yield and growth potential.

- Application: Aim for a moderate dividend yield of 2% to 4% combined with strong dividend growth potential. This balance can provide both current income and long-term capital appreciation.

Reinvesting Dividends for Compounding Growth

One of the most powerful aspects of dividend growth investing is the ability to reinvest dividends to compound your returns. By automatically reinvesting your dividends into additional shares of the same stock, you increase your ownership in the company, which in turn generates more dividends. This compounding effect can lead to exponential growth in your investment over time.

- Application: Use dividend reinvestment plans (DRIPs) to automatically reinvest your dividends. DRIPs allow you to purchase additional shares without paying commissions, accelerating the compounding process and maximizing your returns.

Risks and Considerations in Dividend Investing

While dividend investing offers numerous benefits, it's important to be aware of the risks and considerations associated with this strategy. Understanding these risks will help you make informed decisions and manage your portfolio effectively.

Dividend Cuts and Suspensions

One of the primary risks of dividend investing is the possibility of dividend cuts or suspensions. Companies may reduce or eliminate dividends during periods of financial difficulty, economic downturns, or when they need to conserve cash for other purposes. Dividend cuts can lead to a decline in the stock price and reduce your income stream.

- Mitigation Strategy: To minimize the impact of dividend cuts, diversify your dividend portfolio across multiple sectors and industries. Focus on companies with strong balance sheets, low payout ratios, and a history of maintaining dividends through various economic cycles.

Interest Rate Sensitivity

Dividend-paying stocks, particularly those with higher yields, can be sensitive to changes in interest rates. When interest rates rise, fixed-income investments like bonds become more attractive, potentially leading to a decline in the demand for dividend stocks. This can result in lower stock prices and reduced income from dividends.

- Mitigation Strategy: Maintain a balanced portfolio that includes both dividend-paying stocks and other asset classes, such as bonds, to reduce interest rate risk. Additionally, focus on dividend growth stocks that can continue to increase dividends even in a rising interest rate environment.

Sector Concentration

Dividend-paying stocks are often concentrated in certain sectors, such as utilities, consumer staples, and real estate. While these sectors can provide stable income, they may also be vulnerable to sector-specific risks, such as regulatory changes, commodity price fluctuations, or economic shifts.

- Mitigation Strategy: Diversify your dividend portfolio across multiple sectors to reduce the impact of

sector-specific risks. Include dividend-paying stocks from a variety of industries, such as technology, healthcare, and finance, to enhance diversification and reduce overall risk.

Valuation Risk

Investing in dividend stocks that are overvalued can limit your potential returns and increase the risk of capital loss. High valuations may be driven by investor demand for income, leading to inflated stock prices that are not supported by the company's fundamentals.

- Mitigation Strategy: Conduct thorough research and valuation analysis before purchasing dividend stocks. Focus on companies with reasonable valuations, strong fundamentals, and growth potential. Consider using valuation metrics such as the price-to-earnings (P/E) ratio, price-to-book (P/B) ratio, and dividend yield to assess whether a stock is fairly valued.

Inflation Risk

Inflation can erode the purchasing power of your dividend income, especially if the dividend growth rate does not keep pace with inflation. This is particularly important for retirees or those relying on dividends for income, as rising costs can reduce the real value of their income stream.

- Mitigation Strategy: Invest in dividend growth stocks that have a history of increasing dividends at a rate higher than inflation. Companies with strong pricing power, such as those in consumer staples or healthcare, may be better positioned to maintain and grow dividends during periods of inflation.

Conclusion: Harnessing the Power of Dividend Investing

Dividend investing is a powerful strategy that can provide a steady stream of income, long-term growth, and a measure of stability to your portfolio. By focusing on high-quality dividend-paying stocks and dividend growers, you can build a portfolio that offers both income and capital appreciation, helping you achieve your financial goals.

As a Minimalistic Entrepreneur, dividend investing aligns with your goal of building wealth over time while managing risk. By understanding the benefits, risks, and strategies associated with dividend investing, you can make informed decisions that support your long-term financial success.

Remember, the key to successful dividend investing is patience, discipline, and a focus on quality. Stay committed to your investment strategy, reinvest your dividends, and regularly review your portfolio to ensure it remains aligned with your financial objectives. With a well-structured dividend portfolio, you'll enjoy the benefits of passive income, compounding growth, and the peace of mind that comes from investing in stable, financially strong companies.

Growth Investing

As you continue to develop and refine your investment strategy, you may be drawn to the potential of growth investing. Growth investing focuses on identifying and investing in companies that are expected to grow at an above-average rate compared to other companies or the overall market. These companies, often leaders in innovation or those in rapidly expanding industries, have the potential to deliver significant returns over time, making growth investing an attractive strategy for investors looking to maximize their wealth.

In this part, we'll explore the intricacies of growth investing, including how to identify high-growth potential stocks, evaluate key growth metrics, and strike a balance between growth and value. By the end of this chapter, you'll be equipped with the knowledge and tools to incorporate growth investing into your portfolio, allowing you to capitalize on opportunities in the stock market while managing the associated risks.

Identifying High-Growth Potential Stocks: Where to Look for Tomorrow's Winners

The first step in growth investing is identifying companies with the potential for significant future growth. These companies are often found in sectors that are experiencing rapid expansion, driven by technological innovation, changing consumer behaviors, or emerging markets. While growth stocks can be found across various industries, they share common characteristics that signal their potential for outperformance.

Key Characteristics of High-Growth Stocks

1. Strong Revenue Growth:

Companies with high-growth potential typically exhibit strong and consistent revenue growth. This growth is often driven by increasing demand for the company's products or services, expansion into new markets, or the introduction of innovative solutions that disrupt existing industries.

- Application: Look for companies that have demonstrated consistent year-over-year revenue growth, particularly those that have maintained or accelerated their growth rates over multiple quarters or years. High revenue growth is often a sign that the company is capturing market share and positioning itself for continued expansion.

2. Innovative Products and Services:

High-growth companies are often at the forefront of innovation, offering products or services that meet new or evolving consumer needs. These companies may operate in sectors such as technology, healthcare, or renewable energy, where innovation is a key driver of growth.

- Application: Focus on companies that are leaders in their respective industries, particularly those with a strong track record of innovation. Consider the company's product pipeline, research and development efforts, and the potential impact of its innovations on the market.

3. Expanding Market Opportunities:

Growth companies often operate in industries or regions with significant growth potential. This could include emerging markets, sectors undergoing digital transformation, or industries benefiting from favorable demographic trends.

- Application: Identify companies that are expanding into new markets or segments, particularly those with untapped potential. Consider factors such as population growth, increasing consumer spending, and technological adoption when evaluating market opportunities.

4. Scalable Business Model:

A scalable business model allows a company to grow rapidly without a corresponding increase in costs. High-growth companies often have scalable operations, enabling them to expand efficiently and increase profitability as they grow.

- Application: Look for companies with a scalable business model, such as those with low marginal costs or the ability to leverage technology to reach a larger customer base. Scalability is a key factor in sustaining high growth rates over time.

5. Strong Management Team:

A capable and visionary management team is crucial to a company's ability to execute its growth strategy. Companies with high-growth potential are often led by experienced leaders with a proven track record of driving growth and navigating challenges.

- Application: Research the backgrounds and accomplishments of the company's management team. Consider their experience in the industry, previous successes, and their ability to articulate and execute a clear growth strategy.

Sectors and Industries to Watch

While high-growth companies can be found across various sectors, some industries are particularly known for their growth potential. Here are a few sectors to watch when searching for growth opportunities:

1. Technology: The technology sector is synonymous with growth, driven by constant innovation and the rapid adoption of new technologies. Companies in this sector often lead the way in areas such as cloud computing, artificial intelligence, e-commerce, and cybersecurity.

2. Healthcare: The healthcare sector offers significant growth potential, particularly in areas such as biotechnology, pharmaceuticals, and medical devices. Advances in research, aging populations, and increasing demand for healthcare services contribute to the growth of this sector.

3. Renewable Energy: The shift toward sustainable energy sources is creating growth opportunities in the renewable energy sector. Companies involved in solar, wind, and battery storage technologies are poised to benefit from the global transition to clean energy.

4. Consumer Discretionary: Companies in the consumer discretionary sector, including those in e-commerce, entertainment, and luxury goods, can experience rapid growth driven by changing consumer preferences and increasing disposable income.

5. Financial Technology (FinTech): The FinTech sector is disrupting traditional financial services through innovations such as digital payments, blockchain, and online lending platforms. Companies in this sector are often at the forefront of the digital transformation of finance.

Evaluating Growth Metrics: The Numbers That Matter

Once you've identified potential high-growth companies, the next step is to evaluate their growth metrics to determine whether they are worthy additions to your portfolio. Growth metrics provide insights into a company's financial health, profitability, and future growth prospects. Here are the key metrics to consider:

1. Earnings Per Share (EPS) Growth:

Earnings per share (EPS) growth is a critical metric for growth investors. It measures the company's profitability on a per-share basis and indicates how effectively the company is growing its earnings relative to its outstanding shares.

   - Application: Look for companies with consistent and strong EPS growth, particularly those that have exceeded analyst expectations. High EPS growth is a sign that the company is increasing its profitability and delivering value to shareholders.

2. Revenue Growth Rate:

The revenue growth rate measures the percentage increase in a company's revenue over a specific period, typically on a quarterly or annual basis. A high revenue growth rate is a key indicator of a company's ability to expand its market presence and drive sales.

   - Application: Focus on companies with double-digit revenue growth rates, particularly those that have maintained or accelerated their growth over time. Consistent revenue growth is essential for sustaining long-term earnings growth and capital appreciation.

3. Price-to-Earnings (P/E) Ratio:

The price-to-earnings (P/E) ratio is a valuation metric that compares a company's stock price to its earnings per share. While growth stocks often have higher P/E ratios due to their strong growth potential, it's important to assess whether the P/E ratio is justified by the company's future earnings prospects.

- Application: Compare the P/E ratio of the growth stock to its peers and the broader market. A higher P/E ratio may be acceptable for a company with exceptional growth prospects, but be cautious of excessively high valuations that may not be sustainable.

4. Price-to-Earnings-Growth (PEG) Ratio:

The price-to-earnings-growth (PEG) ratio is a variation of the P/E ratio that takes into account the company's earnings growth rate. The PEG ratio is calculated by dividing the P/E ratio by the annual EPS growth rate. It provides a more comprehensive view of a company's valuation relative to its growth potential.

- Application: A PEG ratio below 1.0 is generally considered attractive, indicating that the stock may be undervalued relative to its growth prospects. However, consider the context of the industry and the company's growth trajectory when evaluating the PEG ratio.

5. Return on Equity (ROE):

Return on equity (ROE) measures a company's profitability by calculating the return generated on shareholders' equity. A high ROE indicates that the company is effectively using its equity base to generate profits, which is particularly important for growth companies.

- Application: Focus on companies with a high and improving ROE, particularly those with ROE levels above the industry average. Strong ROE is often a sign of efficient management and a sustainable competitive advantage.

6. Free Cash Flow (FCF):

Free cash flow (FCF) is the cash generated by a company after accounting for capital expenditures. It's a key indicator of a company's financial health and its ability to fund future growth, pay dividends, or repurchase shares.

- Application: Look for companies with positive and growing FCF. Companies with strong FCF have the flexibility to invest in growth initiatives, reduce debt, or return capital to shareholders, all of which can contribute to long-term value creation.

7. Debt-to-Equity Ratio:

The debt-to-equity ratio measures the company's financial leverage by comparing its total debt to shareholders' equity. While some debt can be beneficial for growth, excessive leverage can increase financial risk, particularly for growth companies that may need to invest heavily in expansion.

- Application: Assess the company's debt-to-equity ratio relative to its peers and the industry average. Look for companies with manageable levels of debt that are capable of servicing their obligations while continuing to invest in growth.

Balancing Growth and Value: The Art of Strategic Investing

While growth investing offers the potential for substantial returns, it's important to strike a balance between growth and value in your portfolio. Growth stocks, by their nature, tend to have higher volatility and risk compared to value stocks, which are typically more stable and offer lower but consistent returns. Balancing growth and value can help you capture the upside of high-growth opportunities while maintaining a degree of stability and risk management in your portfolio.

Why Balance Matters

Balancing growth and value allows you to take advantage of different market conditions and reduce the overall risk of your portfolio. Growth stocks may outperform during bull markets when investor optimism is high, while value stocks may provide stability and income during market downturns or periods of economic uncertainty.

Strategies for Balancing Growth and Value

1. Core and Satellite Approach:

The core and satellite approach involves building a diversified portfolio with a core of stable, value-oriented investments and a satellite of high-growth stocks. The core provides a foundation of stability and income, while the satellite offers the potential for higher returns through growth investments.

- Application: Allocate a significant portion of your portfolio to value-oriented investments, such as blue-chip stocks, dividend-paying companies, and bonds. Complement this core with a selection of high-growth stocks that have the potential for significant capital appreciation.

2. Risk Management through Diversification:

Diversification is key to managing the risks associated with growth investing. By spreading your investments across different sectors, industries, and geographic regions, you can reduce the impact of any single investment's poor performance on your overall portfolio.

- Application: Diversify your growth investments across multiple sectors, such as technology, healthcare, and consumer discretionary. This approach helps mitigate sector-specific risks and increases your exposure to various growth opportunities.

3. Periodic Rebalancing:

Over time, the performance of your growth and value investments may cause your portfolio's asset allocation to drift from its original target. Periodic rebalancing ensures that your portfolio remains aligned with your risk tolerance and investment goals.

- Application: Set a regular schedule for rebalancing your portfolio, such as annually or semi-annually. During rebalancing, consider reducing exposure to overperforming growth stocks and reallocating to undervalued or stable investments to maintain your desired balance between growth and value.

4. Dynamic Allocation:

Dynamic allocation involves adjusting your portfolio's balance between growth and value based on market conditions and your investment horizon.

This approach allows you to be more aggressive during favorable market conditions and more conservative during periods of uncertainty.

- Application: Consider increasing your allocation to growth stocks during bull markets or when you have a long investment horizon. Conversely, shift toward value-oriented investments during bear markets or as you approach your financial goals, such as retirement.

Conclusion: Mastering Growth Investing

Growth investing offers the potential for significant wealth creation, but it requires careful research, disciplined evaluation, and strategic balance. By identifying high-growth potential stocks, evaluating key growth metrics, and balancing growth with value, you can harness the power of growth investing to achieve your financial goals.

As a Minimalistic Entrepreneur, growth investing aligns with your desire to maximize returns while managing risk. By staying focused on quality, maintaining a diversified portfolio, and practicing disciplined rebalancing, you can navigate the challenges of growth investing and build a portfolio that delivers both capital appreciation and long-term financial security.

Remember, growth investing is not just about chasing the highest returns—it's about making informed, strategic decisions that align with your long-term objectives. With patience, discipline, and a commitment to continuous learning, you can master the art of growth investing and unlock new opportunities for wealth creation.

Sector and Thematic Investing

As you refine your investment strategy and seek to optimize your portfolio, it becomes increasingly important to consider how you allocate your investments across different market sectors and themes. Sector and thematic investing offers a targeted approach to capturing growth opportunities by focusing on specific areas of the market that are poised for expansion due to economic, technological, or societal trends. This strategy allows you to align your investments with long-term trends and themes that you believe will shape the future, potentially leading to significant returns.

In this part, we'll explore the principles of sector and thematic investing, how to identify long-term trends, and the steps to building a thematic portfolio. By the end of this chapter, you'll have a clear understanding of how to incorporate these strategies into your overall investment approach, enabling you to capitalize on emerging opportunities while maintaining a well-diversified portfolio.

Understanding Market Sectors: The Building Blocks of a Diversified Portfolio

The stock market is divided into various sectors, each representing a broad category of companies that operate within the same industry or share similar characteristics. Understanding these sectors is crucial for investors, as different sectors respond differently to economic cycles, technological advancements, and other market forces.

The Major Market Sectors

1. Technology:

The technology sector includes companies involved in the development and production of technology products and services. This sector is known for its innovation and rapid growth, driven by advancements in software, hardware, telecommunications, and digital services.
- Key Characteristics: High growth potential, innovation-driven, significant research and development (R&D) investments.

- Examples: Apple, Microsoft, Google (Alphabet).

2. Healthcare:

The healthcare sector encompasses companies that provide medical services, manufacture medical equipment or drugs, and support healthcare facilities. This sector is often seen as defensive, as demand for healthcare services remains stable regardless of economic conditions.
- Key Characteristics: Stability, essential services, significant regulatory oversight.
- Examples: Johnson & Johnson, Pfizer, UnitedHealth Group.

3. Financials:

The financial sector includes banks, insurance companies, investment firms, and real estate companies. This sector is closely tied to economic activity, as financial institutions facilitate lending, investment, and risk management.
- Key Characteristics: Sensitivity to interest rates, cyclical nature, dividend-paying.
- Examples: JPMorgan Chase, Goldman Sachs, Berkshire Hathaway.

4. Consumer Discretionary:

The consumer discretionary sector includes companies that sell non-essential goods and services, such as automobiles, apparel, and entertainment. This sector is heavily influenced by consumer spending and economic cycles.
- Key Characteristics: Cyclical, consumer-driven, brand loyalty.
- Examples: Amazon, Tesla, Nike.

5. Consumer Staples:

The consumer staples sector consists of companies that produce essential goods, such as food, beverages, and household products. This sector is considered defensive, as demand for these products remains relatively stable during economic downturns.
- Key Characteristics: Stability, essential goods, recession-resistant.

- Examples: Procter & Gamble, Coca-Cola, Walmart.

6. Energy:

The energy sector includes companies involved in the production and distribution of energy, such as oil, gas, and renewable energy sources. This sector is highly sensitive to commodity prices and geopolitical events.
   - Key Characteristics: Commodity-driven, cyclical, capital-intensive.
   - Examples: ExxonMobil, Chevron, NextEra Energy.

7. Industrials:

The industrials sector encompasses companies involved in manufacturing, construction, and transportation. This sector is closely tied to economic growth and infrastructure development.
   - Key Characteristics: Cyclical, capital-intensive, broad industry scope.
   - Examples: General Electric, Caterpillar, Boeing.

8. Utilities:

The utilities sector includes companies that provide essential services such as electricity, water, and natural gas. This sector is known for its stability and reliable dividend payments.
   - Key Characteristics: Defensive, regulated, stable cash flows.
   - Examples: Duke Energy, Southern Company, Dominion Energy.

9. Real Estate:

The real estate sector consists of companies that develop, own, and operate properties. This sector includes Real Estate Investment Trusts (REITs), which provide investors with exposure to the real estate market.
   - Key Characteristics: Income-generating, interest rate sensitivity, tangible assets.
   - Examples: Simon Property Group, American Tower, Realty Income.

10. Materials:

The materials sector includes companies that produce raw materials such as metals, chemicals, and building products. This sector is sensitive to economic cycles and global demand.

- Key Characteristics: Cyclical, commodity-driven, essential for manufacturing.

- Examples: Dow Inc., DuPont, Newmont Corporation.

11. Communication Services:

The communication services sector includes companies that provide telecommunication, media, and entertainment services. This sector has evolved with the rise of digital communication and streaming platforms.

- Key Characteristics: Growth-oriented, technology-driven, consumer engagement.

- Examples: AT&T, Netflix, Facebook (Meta Platforms).

Sector Rotation: Navigating Economic Cycles

Understanding how different sectors perform during various phases of the economic cycle is key to sector investing. Sector rotation is a strategy where investors shift their investments from one sector to another based on their expectations of economic conditions. For example:

- During an economic expansion, sectors like technology, consumer discretionary, and financials tend to outperform as businesses invest in growth and consumers increase spending.

- During an economic downturn, defensive sectors like consumer staples, healthcare, and utilities often perform better as demand for essential goods and services remains stable.

Application: To implement sector rotation in your portfolio, stay informed about economic indicators such as GDP growth, interest rates, and consumer confidence. Adjust your sector allocations based on the current and anticipated phase of the economic cycle.

Identifying Long-Term Trends: Capitalizing on Thematic Investing

Thematic investing is a strategy that focuses on long-term, structural trends that have the potential to reshape industries, economies, and societies. These trends often transcend individual sectors and are driven by factors such as technological innovation, demographic shifts, and environmental changes. Thematic investing allows you to align your portfolio with these powerful forces, capturing growth opportunities as they unfold over time.

Key Themes in Thematic Investing

Here are some of the most compelling themes in the current investment landscape:

1. Technology and Digital Transformation:

The rapid advancement of technology continues to drive significant changes across industries. The digital transformation theme encompasses trends such as artificial intelligence (AI), cloud computing, cybersecurity, and the Internet of Things (IoT). Companies that are leaders in digital innovation are well-positioned to benefit from this ongoing shift.

- Application: Invest in companies that are at the forefront of digital transformation, particularly those that provide essential technology infrastructure or lead in innovation. Consider technology-focused ETFs or individual stocks in sectors like software, semiconductors, and digital services.

2. Sustainability and Green Energy:

The global transition to a more sustainable economy is creating opportunities in renewable energy, electric vehicles, and environmental protection. The sustainability theme includes companies involved in clean energy production, energy efficiency, and waste management.

- Application: Focus on companies that are leaders in green technology and renewable energy. Consider investments in solar, wind, and battery storage companies, as well as those that are actively reducing their carbon footprint.

3. Healthcare Innovation:

Advances in medical technology, biotechnology, and pharmaceuticals are driving growth in the healthcare sector. The healthcare innovation theme includes companies that are developing cutting-edge treatments, medical devices, and diagnostic tools.

- Application: Invest in companies that are pioneers in healthcare innovation, particularly those with strong R&D pipelines and the potential to bring new therapies to market. Consider healthcare-focused ETFs or individual stocks in biotech and medical device companies.

4. Aging Population:

The global aging population is creating demand for products and services tailored to older adults. The aging population theme includes companies that provide healthcare, financial services, and consumer products designed for this demographic.

- Application: Focus on companies that cater to the needs of an aging population, such as healthcare providers, pharmaceutical companies, and retirement planning services. Consider investing in sectors like healthcare, financial services, and consumer staples.

5. Urbanization and Infrastructure Development:

The growth of urban populations, particularly in emerging markets, is driving demand for infrastructure development, including transportation, housing, and utilities. The urbanization theme includes companies involved in construction, real estate, and infrastructure financing.

- Application: Invest in companies that are positioned to benefit from urbanization and infrastructure projects, particularly those with exposure to emerging markets. Consider real estate investment trusts (REITs), construction firms, and utility companies.

6. Globalization and Emerging Markets:

The continued integration of global economies presents opportunities in emerging markets, where rapid economic growth and rising consumer spending are driving demand. The globalization theme includes companies with significant exposure to emerging markets and those that benefit from international trade.

- Application: Focus on companies with a strong presence in emerging markets or those that are well-positioned to benefit from global trade. Consider emerging market ETFs or individual stocks in multinational corporations.

Building a Thematic Portfolio: A Strategic Approach

Constructing a thematic portfolio involves selecting investments that align with one or more of the themes identified above. This approach allows you to concentrate your investments in areas where you believe the most significant growth opportunities lie. However, thematic investing requires careful planning and consideration to ensure that your portfolio remains diversified and aligned with your risk tolerance.

Steps to Building a Thematic Portfolio

1. Define Your Investment Themes:

Begin by identifying the themes that resonate most with your investment philosophy and long-term outlook. Consider the potential impact of each theme on various sectors and industries, and assess the opportunities for growth.

- Application: Choose two or three key themes that align with your beliefs about the future. For example, if you believe in the continued rise of digital technology and the shift toward sustainability, you might focus on the themes of digital transformation and green energy.

2. Select the Right Investments:

Once you've defined your themes, the next step is to select investments that provide exposure to these themes. This could include individual stocks, exchange-traded funds (ETFs), or mutual funds that are specifically designed to track the performance of a particular theme.

- Application: Use thematic ETFs as a way to gain broad exposure to a specific theme. These ETFs are often diversified across multiple companies within the theme, reducing the risk associated with investing in individual stocks. Additionally, consider selecting individual stocks that are leaders within the theme and have strong growth potential.

3. Diversify Across Themes and Sectors:

While thematic investing focuses on specific trends, it's essential to maintain diversification to manage risk. Ensure that your thematic portfolio is diversified across different sectors and industries, even within a single theme. This reduces the impact of any one company or sector underperforming.

- Application: Diversify your thematic investments by selecting companies or ETFs that represent different aspects of the theme. For example, within the green energy theme, you might invest in companies involved in solar energy, wind energy, and energy storage to spread your risk.

4. Monitor and Adjust Your Portfolio:

Thematic investing requires active management, as themes can evolve over time. Regularly review your portfolio to ensure that your investments remain aligned with your themes and that the themes themselves continue to hold long-term growth potential.

- Application: Set a schedule for reviewing your thematic portfolio, such as quarterly or semi-annually. During these reviews, assess the performance of your investments, make adjustments as needed, and stay informed about any developments that could impact the themes you're investing in.

5. Consider the Long-Term Horizon:

Thematic investing is often a long-term strategy, as the trends it targets can take years or even decades to fully materialize. Be prepared to hold your thematic investments for the long term, and avoid the temptation to react to short-term market fluctuations.

- Application: Stay committed to your investment themes and resist the urge to make frequent changes based on short-term news or market volatility. Keep your focus on the long-term potential of the themes you've identified and trust in your research and analysis.

Conclusion: Embracing Sector and Thematic Investing

Sector and thematic investing offers a powerful way to target specific areas of the market that are poised for growth, allowing you to align your portfolio with your beliefs about the future. By understanding market sectors, identifying long-term trends, and building a diversified thematic portfolio, you can capitalize on emerging opportunities while managing risk.

As a Minimalistic Entrepreneur, sector and thematic investing enables you to take a more focused and strategic approach to building wealth. By concentrating your investments in areas that you believe will drive future growth, you can enhance your returns and create a portfolio that reflects your vision for the future.

Remember, successful sector and thematic investing requires careful research, disciplined execution, and a long-term perspective. Stay informed about the trends shaping the world, regularly review your portfolio, and be prepared to adapt your strategy as new opportunities arise. With the right approach, sector and thematic investing can be a powerful tool in your journey toward financial independence and lasting wealth.

CHAPTER NINE

MONITORING AND REBALANCING YOUR PORTFOLIO

Regular Portfolio Review

Investing is not a one-time activity; it's an ongoing process that requires regular attention and adjustments to ensure that your portfolio remains aligned with your financial goals. As a Minimalistic Entrepreneur, one of the most critical aspects of your investment strategy is the regular review and rebalancing of your portfolio. This process helps you stay on track, manage risk, and optimize returns over time.

In this part, we'll explore the importance of setting regular review schedules, identify key performance indicators (KPIs) to track, and discuss how to leverage portfolio management tools to streamline this process. By the end of this chapter, you'll have a clear understanding of how to monitor your investments effectively and make informed decisions that will help you achieve long-term financial success.

Setting Review Schedules: The Foundation of Effective Portfolio Management

Regularly reviewing your portfolio is essential for maintaining alignment with your investment objectives and adjusting to changes in market conditions or your personal financial situation. Establishing a consistent review schedule ensures that you stay proactive in managing your investments rather than reacting to market volatility or unforeseen events.

Why Regular Reviews Matter

Regular portfolio reviews serve several important purposes:

1. Staying Aligned with Goals:

Your financial goals may evolve over time due to changes in your personal circumstances, such as a new job, marriage, or nearing retirement. Regular reviews help ensure that your portfolio continues to reflect your current objectives and risk tolerance.

2. Managing Risk:

As the market fluctuates, the allocation of assets in your portfolio can drift away from your target allocation, potentially increasing your risk. Regular reviews allow you to rebalance your portfolio to maintain your desired level of risk.

3. Optimizing Performance:

Monitoring your portfolio's performance helps you identify underperforming assets or sectors and make adjustments to optimize returns. It also provides an opportunity to take advantage of new investment opportunities that align with your strategy.

4. Tax Planning:

Regular reviews can help you identify opportunities for tax-loss harvesting, where you sell underperforming investments to offset capital gains, or tax-gain harvesting, where you realize gains in a lower tax bracket.

How Often Should You Review Your Portfolio?

The frequency of your portfolio reviews depends on several factors, including your investment horizon, risk tolerance, and the complexity of your portfolio. However, there are general guidelines you can follow:

1. Quarterly Reviews:

For most investors, a quarterly review is sufficient to stay on top of your portfolio's performance and make necessary adjustments. Quarterly reviews allow you to track progress, rebalance as needed, and respond to any significant market developments.

- Application: Set a specific date each quarter to review your portfolio. This could be at the end of March, June, September, and December, or another schedule that aligns with your financial planning calendar.

2. Annual Comprehensive Review:

In addition to quarterly reviews, conduct a more comprehensive annual review. This review should involve a deeper analysis of your portfolio's performance over the year, an assessment of your financial goals, and any changes in your personal circumstances.

- Application: Schedule your annual review at the beginning of the year to set the tone for your investment strategy. During this review, revisit your long-term goals, assess your risk tolerance, and evaluate the overall health of your portfolio.

3. Ad Hoc Reviews:

In certain situations, you may need to conduct an ad hoc review of your portfolio. Significant life events, such as receiving an inheritance, changing jobs, or a major market correction, may warrant a more immediate review to assess the impact on your investments.

- Application: Be prepared to review your portfolio outside of your regular schedule if a major event occurs. However, avoid the temptation to react to every market fluctuation; instead, focus on events that have a meaningful impact on your financial situation.

Key Performance Indicators to Track: Measuring Your Portfolio's Success

To effectively review your portfolio, it's essential to track key performance indicators (KPIs) that provide insights into how well your investments are performing. These KPIs help you assess whether your portfolio is on track to meet your goals and whether any adjustments are necessary.

1. Portfolio Return

The most basic KPI to track is your portfolio's overall return, which measures the percentage gain or loss of your investments over a specific period. Comparing your portfolio's return to relevant benchmarks, such as the S&P 500 or a blended index that matches your asset allocation, can help you assess your performance relative to the broader market.

- Application: Calculate your portfolio's return on a quarterly and annual basis, and compare it to your benchmark. If your portfolio consistently underperforms the benchmark, it may be time to re-evaluate your investment strategy or consider reallocating assets.

2. Asset Allocation

Asset allocation is the distribution of your investments across different asset classes, such as stocks, bonds, real estate, and cash. Over time, market movements can cause your allocation to drift from your target, potentially increasing your risk or reducing your potential returns.

- Application: Regularly compare your current asset allocation to your target allocation. If there are significant discrepancies, rebalance your portfolio by selling overperforming assets and buying underperforming ones to restore balance.

3. Risk-Adjusted Return

Risk-adjusted return measures how much return you're getting for the level of risk you're taking. Common metrics include the Sharpe ratio, which compares your portfolio's excess return (return above the risk-free rate) to its volatility. A higher Sharpe ratio indicates better risk-adjusted performance.

- Application: Calculate the Sharpe ratio or other risk-adjusted metrics to evaluate whether you're being adequately compensated for the risk you're taking. If your risk-adjusted return is low, consider adjusting your asset allocation or selecting investments with a better risk-reward profile.

4. Diversification

Diversification is a key strategy for managing risk, but it's important to regularly assess how well-diversified your portfolio truly is. Over time, certain assets may become overconcentrated due to market movements, increasing your exposure to specific sectors or companies.

- Application: Analyze the concentration of your investments across different asset classes, sectors, and geographies. Ensure that no single investment or sector dominates your portfolio, and make adjustments to enhance diversification if necessary.

5. Dividend Yield and Income

For investors who rely on dividends for income, tracking the dividend yield of your portfolio is crucial. The dividend yield is the annual dividend income divided by the current market value of your portfolio. Monitoring this KPI helps ensure that your income needs are being met.

- Application: Calculate the dividend yield of your portfolio and compare it to your income goals. If the yield falls short, consider reallocating to higher-yielding assets or adjusting your income expectations.

6. Expense Ratios and Fees

Investment fees can significantly impact your overall returns, especially over the long term. Regularly reviewing the expense ratios of your mutual funds or ETFs, as well as any management fees, helps you identify opportunities to reduce costs.

- Application: Track the expense ratios of your investments and compare them to industry averages. If you're paying above-average fees, consider switching to lower-cost alternatives, such as index funds or ETFs, to improve your net returns.

7. Tax Efficiency

Tax efficiency is an important consideration for optimizing your after-tax returns. This includes tracking capital gains, dividend income, and any tax-loss harvesting opportunities to minimize your tax liability.

- Application: Review your portfolio's tax implications, particularly at year-end, to identify opportunities for tax-loss harvesting or adjusting your investment strategy to improve tax efficiency. Consider using tax-efficient funds or holding tax-inefficient investments in tax-advantaged accounts.

Using Portfolio Management Tools: Streamlining the Review Process

Managing a portfolio can be complex, especially as it grows in size and diversification. Fortunately, there are numerous portfolio management tools available that can help you monitor your investments, track performance, and make informed decisions.

1. Online Brokerage Platforms

Many online brokerage platforms offer built-in portfolio management tools that provide real-time data, performance tracking, and analysis. These tools can help you monitor your portfolio's return, asset allocation, and risk metrics, all in one place.

- Application: Take advantage of the portfolio management features offered by your brokerage platform. Use these tools to set alerts for significant changes in your portfolio, track your performance against benchmarks, and access research and analysis to inform your decisions.

2. Financial Planning Software

Financial planning software, such as Personal Capital, Mint, or Quicken, provides a comprehensive view of your financial situation, including your investments. These tools allow you to track your portfolio's performance, assess your progress toward financial goals, and manage cash flow and budgeting.

- Application: Integrate your investment accounts into financial planning software to gain a holistic view of your finances. Use the software's reporting and analysis features to conduct regular portfolio reviews and adjust your investment strategy as needed.

3. Robo-Advisors

Robo-advisors are automated investment platforms that use algorithms to create and manage portfolios based on your risk tolerance and financial goals. These platforms offer ongoing portfolio monitoring, automatic rebalancing, and tax-loss harvesting, making them a convenient option for hands-off investors.

- Application: Consider using a robo-advisor if you prefer a more automated approach to portfolio management. While robo-advisors handle most of the heavy lifting, it's still important to conduct periodic reviews to ensure that the platform's strategy aligns with your evolving goals.

4. Spreadsheets and Custom Trackers

For those who prefer a more hands-on approach, creating a custom spreadsheet or tracker can provide a tailored solution for portfolio management. Spreadsheets allow you to track specific KPIs, model different scenarios, and perform detailed analysis of your investments.

- Application:
Develop a spreadsheet that tracks your portfolio's performance, asset allocation, risk metrics, and expenses. Customize the spreadsheet to include the KPIs most relevant to your strategy, and update it regularly to stay on top of your investments.

Conclusion: The Power of Regular Portfolio Review

Regularly reviewing and rebalancing your portfolio is essential to maintaining alignment with your financial goals, managing risk, and optimizing performance. By setting a consistent review schedule, tracking key performance indicators, and leveraging portfolio management tools, you can stay proactive in managing your investments and ensure that your portfolio remains on track.

As a Minimalistic Entrepreneur, the discipline of regular portfolio review is a critical component of your investment strategy. It allows you to adapt to changing market conditions, take advantage of new opportunities, and make informed decisions that support your long-term financial success.

Remember, investing is a journey, not a destination. Regularly reviewing and adjusting your portfolio is part of that journey, helping you navigate the ups and downs of the market with confidence and clarity. By staying engaged with your investments and committed to your goals, you'll be well-equipped to build and maintain a portfolio that reflects your values, aspirations, and financial objectives.

When to Buy, Hold, or Sell

One of the most challenging aspects of investing is knowing when to buy, hold, or sell your investments. These decisions can have a significant impact on your portfolio's performance and your long-term financial goals. As a Minimalistic Entrepreneur, it's essential to develop clear criteria for making these decisions, recognize red flags that may signal it's time to sell, and avoid common mistakes that many investors make when buying or selling stocks.

In this part, we'll explore how to develop a disciplined approach to buying, holding, and selling investments. You'll learn how to establish clear decision-making criteria, identify red flags that warrant action, and avoid emotional pitfalls that can lead to poor investment outcomes. By the end of this chapter, you'll be better equipped to make informed decisions that align with your investment strategy and long-term objectives.

Developing Clear Criteria for Decisions: The Foundation of Strategic Investing

The key to successful investing lies in developing a clear, well-defined set of criteria that guides your buy, hold, and sell decisions. These criteria should be based on your investment strategy, financial goals, and risk tolerance, and they should be consistently applied to avoid emotional decision-making.

1. Criteria for Buying Investments

The decision to buy an investment should be based on a thorough analysis of its potential to contribute to your portfolio's growth and stability. Here's how to develop criteria for making informed buy decisions:

- Fundamental Analysis: Before buying a stock, conduct a fundamental analysis to evaluate the company's financial health, profitability, and growth prospects. Look at key metrics such as revenue growth, earnings per share (EPS), return on equity (ROE), and free cash flow. Ensure that the company has a strong balance sheet, a sustainable business model, and a competitive advantage in its industry.

- Valuation: Consider whether the stock is fairly valued based on its price-to-earnings (P/E) ratio, price-to-book (P/B) ratio, and other valuation metrics. Avoid overpaying for a stock, even if it has strong growth potential. Look for opportunities to buy high-quality companies at a discount to their intrinsic value.

- Growth Potential: Assess the company's growth potential based on its market position, innovation, and ability to capitalize on industry trends. Companies with strong growth potential often operate in expanding industries or have a track record of successfully entering new markets.

- Dividend Yield (if applicable): If you're focused on income, consider the stock's dividend yield and its history of dividend payments. Look for companies with a stable or growing dividend, as well as a reasonable payout ratio that suggests the dividend is sustainable.

- Alignment with Investment Goals: Ensure that the stock aligns with your overall investment strategy and long-term goals. For example, if you're focused on growth, prioritize companies with high earnings growth potential. If you're focused on income, prioritize companies with a strong dividend history.

- Risk Assessment: Evaluate the risks associated with the investment, including market risk, industry risk, and company-specific risk. Consider how the stock fits into your portfolio's overall risk profile and whether it complements your existing holdings.

Application: Before buying a stock, ask yourself whether it meets your established criteria. Avoid impulsive decisions based on market hype or short-term price movements. Stick to your strategy and only buy investments that align with your long-term objectives.

2. Criteria for Holding Investments

Once you've added a stock to your portfolio, the decision to hold it should be based on its continued alignment with your investment goals and performance expectations. Holding investments requires discipline, especially during periods of market volatility.

- Performance Tracking: Regularly monitor the stock's performance relative to your expectations and the broader market. If the stock continues to meet or exceed your performance criteria, there's no need to sell. Focus on long-term growth rather than short-term price fluctuations.

- Fundamental Strength: Ensure that the company's fundamentals remain strong. This includes consistent revenue growth, stable or increasing profit margins, and effective management. If the company's fundamentals remain intact, consider holding the stock even during market downturns.

- Dividend Sustainability (if applicable): If you're invested in dividend-paying stocks, monitor the sustainability of the dividend. Look for signs that the company can continue to pay or increase its dividend over time, such as strong cash flow and a reasonable payout ratio.

- Economic and Industry Trends: Consider how broader economic and industry trends may impact the stock. If the company is well-positioned to benefit from these trends, holding the stock may be advantageous. Conversely, if the company's growth prospects are diminishing due to adverse industry trends, it may be time to reassess your position.

- Portfolio Fit: Evaluate how the stock fits within your overall portfolio. Ensure that it contributes to your desired asset allocation, diversification, and risk management. If the stock has become overconcentrated due to significant price appreciation, consider trimming your position to maintain balance.

Application: Develop a checklist of criteria for holding investments and review it regularly. Avoid the temptation to sell based on short-term market noise or emotional reactions. Instead, focus on the stock's long-term potential and its continued alignment with your investment goals.

3. Criteria for Selling Investments

Selling a stock can be one of the most difficult decisions for investors, particularly when emotions come into play. However, there are clear criteria that can guide your decision to sell, ensuring that you take action based on rational analysis rather than impulse.

- Deteriorating Fundamentals: One of the most compelling reasons to sell a stock is when the company's fundamentals begin to deteriorate. This could include declining revenue or earnings, shrinking profit margins, increasing debt levels, or a loss of competitive advantage. If the company's prospects have fundamentally changed for the worse, it may be time to sell.

- Valuation Concerns: If a stock becomes significantly overvalued relative to its intrinsic value or industry peers, it may be a good time to sell. High valuations can lead to inflated expectations and increased risk of a price correction. Consider taking profits if the stock's valuation no longer justifies its growth potential.

- Change in Investment Goals: If your personal circumstances or financial goals have changed, it may necessitate selling certain investments. For example, if you're approaching retirement, you may want to shift from growth-oriented stocks to more income-focused or conservative investments.

- Tax-Loss Harvesting: Selling a stock at a loss can be a strategic move to offset capital gains and reduce your tax liability. If a stock is underperforming and shows no signs of recovery, consider selling it as part of a tax-loss harvesting strategy.

- Portfolio Rebalancing: Over time, certain stocks may become overrepresented in your portfolio due to significant price appreciation. Regularly rebalance your portfolio by selling portions of these positions to maintain your desired asset allocation and reduce risk.

- Ethical or Strategic Concerns: Sometimes, non-financial factors may prompt you to sell a stock. This could include concerns about the company's ethics, management decisions, or changes in its business model that no longer align with your values or investment strategy.

Application: Before selling a stock, ensure that your decision is based on one or more of the criteria outlined above. Avoid selling out of fear or greed, and resist the urge to time the market. Stick to your strategy and make decisions that support your long-term financial goals.

Recognizing Red Flags: Knowing When to Take Action

Recognizing red flags in your investments is crucial for protecting your portfolio from unnecessary risk. Red flags are warning signs that indicate potential problems with a company or its stock, and they may signal the need for closer scrutiny or even selling the investment.

1. Declining Revenue or Earnings

One of the most significant red flags is a sustained decline in revenue or earnings. If a company consistently reports lower sales or profits, it may indicate underlying issues such as lost market share, ineffective management, or changing industry dynamics.

- Action: Investigate the reasons behind the decline. If the issues are temporary and the company has a clear plan for recovery, you may choose to hold. However, if the decline appears to be part of a longer-term trend, consider selling the stock.

2. Negative Changes in Management

Leadership changes can have a profound impact on a company's direction and performance. If key executives, such as the CEO or CFO, resign unexpectedly or if new management implements drastic changes that you disagree with, it could be a red flag.

- Action: Assess the impact of the management changes on the company's strategy and operations. If the new leadership inspires confidence and has a clear plan for growth, you may decide to hold. If not, selling might be the prudent choice.

3. Increasing Debt Levels

A sharp increase in a company's debt levels can be a sign of financial distress. While some debt can be beneficial for growth, excessive leverage increases the risk of default and can lead to a downward spiral if the company cannot generate enough cash flow to service its debt.

- Action: Monitor the company's debt-to-equity ratio and interest coverage ratio. If debt levels become unsustainable, it may be time to sell, especially if the company's growth prospects are weakening.

4. Dividend Cuts or Suspensions

For income-focused investors, a dividend cut or suspension is a major red flag. It often indicates that the company is facing financial difficulties or is prioritizing other uses of cash over returning value to shareholders.

- Action: Reevaluate the investment if the company cuts or suspends its dividend. Consider whether the company's long-term prospects justify holding the stock without the dividend, or if it's better to sell and reinvest in a more reliable income-generating asset.

5. Regulatory or Legal Issues

Companies facing significant regulatory or legal challenges may experience long-term negative impacts on their business. This could include fines, restrictions on operations, or damage to their reputation.

- Action

: Assess the severity and potential impact of the regulatory or legal issues. If they pose a significant threat to the company's future, it may be wise to sell before the situation worsens.

6. Sector or Industry Decline

Sometimes, entire sectors or industries may enter a period of decline due to technological disruption, changing consumer preferences, or adverse regulatory changes. If a company's prospects are tied to a declining industry, it may struggle to grow or maintain profitability.

- Action: Evaluate whether the company can adapt to the changing environment or if it's better to exit the investment. Consider reallocating your capital to sectors or industries with more promising growth prospects.

Avoiding Common Selling Mistakes: Staying Disciplined

Selling investments is fraught with potential pitfalls, many of which are driven by emotions rather than logic. Avoiding these common selling mistakes can help you stay disciplined and make decisions that align with your long-term strategy.

1. Selling in Panic During Market Downturns

One of the most common mistakes investors make is selling in a panic during market downturns. While it's natural to feel anxious when the market is falling, selling in response to short-term volatility often results in locking in losses and missing out on the eventual recovery.

- Solution: Stay calm and focus on your long-term investment strategy. Remember that market downturns are a normal part of the investment cycle, and history shows that markets tend to recover over time. If your investment thesis remains intact, consider holding or even buying more during downturns.

2. Selling Too Early

Another common mistake is selling too early, particularly when a stock has appreciated significantly. While it's tempting to take profits, selling too soon can result in missing out on further gains if the company continues to perform well.

- Solution: Establish clear criteria for when to sell and stick to them. Consider using trailing stop orders to lock in gains while allowing the stock to continue rising. Focus on the company's long-term potential rather than short-term price movements.

3. Trying to Time the Market

Attempting to time the market by predicting short-term price movements is a risky strategy that often leads to suboptimal results. Even experienced investors struggle to consistently time the market accurately.

- Solution: Focus on time in the market rather than timing the market. Stay invested according to your long-term strategy and make decisions based on fundamentals rather than market timing.

4. Ignoring Tax Implications

Selling investments without considering the tax implications can result in a higher tax bill than anticipated. Capital gains taxes can significantly reduce your net returns, especially if you're in a high tax bracket.

- Solution: Consider the tax implications before selling any investment. Utilize tax-efficient strategies such as tax-loss harvesting or holding investments for more than one year to qualify for long-term capital gains tax rates. Consult with a tax advisor if needed.

5. Letting Emotions Drive Decisions

Emotions such as fear, greed, and overconfidence can cloud your judgment and lead to irrational selling decisions. It's important to recognize these emotions and keep them in check to avoid making costly mistakes.

- Solution: Develop a clear, rules-based investment strategy and stick to it. Regularly review your investment decisions to ensure they are based on logic and analysis, not emotions. Consider keeping a journal of your investment decisions and the reasoning behind them to hold yourself accountable.

Conclusion: Mastering the Art of Buying, Holding, and Selling

Knowing when to buy, hold, or sell investments is a critical skill for any investor. By developing clear criteria for these decisions, recognizing red flags that warrant action, and avoiding common selling mistakes, you can stay disciplined and make informed choices that align with your long-term financial goals.

As a Minimalistic Entrepreneur, the ability to make rational, well-considered decisions in the face of market volatility and uncertainty is key to building and maintaining a successful portfolio. Remember that investing is a marathon, not a sprint, and that staying focused on your strategy and long-term objectives will serve you well in the pursuit of financial independence.

By mastering the art of buying, holding, and selling, you'll be better equipped to navigate the complexities of the stock market, capitalize on opportunities, and avoid the pitfalls that derail many investors. Stay disciplined, stay informed, and keep your eye on the ultimate prize: financial freedom and a secure future.

Rebalancing Strategies

As you navigate the journey of investing, maintaining a balanced portfolio is crucial to achieving your long-term financial goals. Over time, market fluctuations can cause your portfolio's asset allocation to drift away from your original plan, potentially increasing your risk or diminishing your returns. Rebalancing is the process of realigning your portfolio to match your desired asset allocation, ensuring that your investments remain aligned with your risk tolerance and financial objectives.

In this part, we'll explore the importance of rebalancing, examine different rebalancing methods, and discuss how often you should rebalance your portfolio. By the end of this chapter, you'll have a clear understanding of how to implement effective rebalancing strategies that will help you maintain a well-diversified and resilient portfolio.

The Importance of Rebalancing: Keeping Your Portfolio on Track

Rebalancing is a critical aspect of portfolio management that helps you maintain control over your investments and manage risk. Without regular rebalancing, your portfolio can become overexposed to certain assets, leading to unintended risks that may not align with your financial goals.

Why Rebalancing Matters

1. Risk Management:

Your asset allocation is the foundation of your investment strategy, reflecting your risk tolerance, time horizon, and financial goals. Over time, market movements can cause certain assets to outperform or underperform, leading to a shift in your portfolio's risk profile. Rebalancing helps you restore your portfolio to its original allocation, ensuring that you're not taking on more risk than you intended.

- Example: If your target allocation is 60% stocks and 40% bonds, but a strong stock market rally causes your portfolio to shift to 70% stocks and 30% bonds, you may be exposed to more volatility than you're comfortable with. Rebalancing would involve selling some of your stock holdings and buying bonds to bring your allocation back to 60/40.

2. Discipline and Consistency:

Rebalancing forces you to follow a disciplined approach to investing, where you buy low and sell high. By selling overperforming assets and buying underperforming ones, you can take advantage of market fluctuations while staying true to your investment strategy.

 - Example: During a market downturn, your bond allocation may increase as stocks decline in value. Rebalancing in this scenario involves selling bonds and buying stocks at lower prices, positioning you to benefit when the market recovers.

3. Avoiding Emotional Decision-Making:

Rebalancing helps you avoid the pitfalls of emotional decision-making by providing a systematic approach to managing your portfolio. Instead of reacting to short-term market movements, rebalancing encourages you to stick to your long-term plan, reducing the likelihood of making impulsive or irrational decisions.

 - Example: If you're tempted to chase recent gains in a particular sector or asset class, rebalancing helps you resist the urge by guiding you to maintain a balanced portfolio that reflects your risk tolerance and goals.

4. Aligning with Financial Goals:

As your financial goals evolve, your asset allocation may need to be adjusted to reflect changes in your risk tolerance, investment horizon, or life circumstances. Rebalancing ensures that your portfolio remains aligned with your current financial objectives, helping you stay on track to achieve your long-term goals.

 - Example: As you approach retirement, you may want to shift your allocation from growth-oriented assets like stocks to more conservative investments like bonds. Rebalancing allows you to gradually adjust your portfolio to match your changing needs.

Different Rebalancing Methods: Choosing the Right Approach

There are several methods for rebalancing your portfolio, each with its own advantages and considerations. The method you choose will depend on your investment strategy, risk tolerance, and personal preferences.

1. Calendar-Based Rebalancing

Calendar-based rebalancing involves rebalancing your portfolio at regular intervals, such as quarterly, semi-annually, or annually. This method is straightforward and easy to implement, as it doesn't require constant monitoring of your portfolio's performance.

- Advantages:
- Simplicity: Calendar-based rebalancing is simple and easy to plan, as you set a fixed schedule for when to rebalance your portfolio.
- Discipline: This method encourages a disciplined approach to investing, reducing the likelihood of emotional decision-making.
- Considerations:
- Market Timing: Since calendar-based rebalancing is based on a fixed schedule, it may not always align with market conditions. You may end up rebalancing at a time when it's not optimal to do so, such as during a period of extreme market volatility.
- Application: If you prefer a straightforward, hands-off approach, calendar-based rebalancing may be a good fit. Set a schedule that aligns with your financial planning calendar, such as the end of each quarter or the beginning of each year.

2. Threshold-Based Rebalancing

Threshold-based rebalancing involves rebalancing your portfolio when your asset allocation deviates from your target allocation by a certain percentage or threshold. For example, you might set a threshold of 5%, meaning you would rebalance your portfolio whenever an asset class exceeds or falls below its target allocation by 5%.

- Advantages:
- Flexibility: Threshold-based rebalancing allows you to respond to significant market movements while avoiding unnecessary transactions

during periods of stability.

- Market Sensitivity: This method ensures that you rebalance only when your portfolio has drifted significantly, helping you stay aligned with your risk tolerance.

- Considerations:

- Complexity: Threshold-based rebalancing requires more frequent monitoring of your portfolio to ensure that you're aware of when the threshold is breached.

- Transaction Costs: More frequent rebalancing may result in higher transaction costs, particularly if your portfolio includes individual stocks or ETFs with trading fees.

- Application: If you prefer a more responsive approach that adjusts to market conditions, threshold-based rebalancing may be suitable. Determine a threshold that reflects your risk tolerance, such as 5% or 10%, and monitor your portfolio regularly to identify when rebalancing is necessary.

3. Cash Flow Rebalancing

Cash flow rebalancing involves using new contributions or withdrawals to bring your portfolio closer to its target allocation. Instead of selling assets to rebalance, you direct new investments (such as regular contributions to a retirement account) or withdrawals (such as during retirement) to the underweighted asset classes.

- Advantages:

- Cost-Effective: Cash flow rebalancing minimizes transaction costs, as you're rebalancing through new contributions or withdrawals rather than selling and buying assets.

- Tax Efficiency: This method reduces the need to sell assets, which can trigger capital gains taxes, making it more tax-efficient.

- Considerations:

- Slow Adjustment: Cash flow rebalancing may take longer to bring your portfolio back to its target allocation, especially if your contributions or withdrawals are small relative to your portfolio's size.

- Limited Control: You may have less control over the timing and magnitude of rebalancing, particularly if your contributions or withdrawals are irregular.

- Application: Cash flow rebalancing is ideal for investors who make regular contributions to their portfolio, such as through a 401(k) or IRA, or for retirees who are making systematic withdrawals. Use this method to gradually bring your portfolio back to its target allocation over time.

4. Tactical Rebalancing

Tactical rebalancing involves making deliberate adjustments to your portfolio based on short-term market opportunities or changes in economic conditions. This method allows for more active management, as you may choose to overweight or underweight certain asset classes based on your market outlook.

- Advantages:

- Potential for Enhanced Returns: Tactical rebalancing allows you to capitalize on market opportunities and potentially enhance your returns by adjusting your allocation in response to changing conditions.

- Flexibility: This method provides greater flexibility to adjust your portfolio based on your views of market trends, economic data, or geopolitical events.

- Considerations:

- Higher Risk: Tactical rebalancing involves a higher level of risk, as it requires market timing and may lead to suboptimal decisions if your predictions are incorrect.

- Increased Complexity: This method requires a deep understanding of market dynamics and frequent monitoring of economic indicators, making it more complex and time-consuming.

- Application: Tactical rebalancing is suited for experienced investors who are comfortable with active management and have a strong understanding of market trends. Use this method selectively to take advantage of specific opportunities, but remain disciplined and avoid overtrading.

Frequency of Rebalancing: Finding the Right Balance

The frequency of rebalancing your portfolio is a critical factor that can impact both your returns and your costs. Rebalancing too frequently can lead to unnecessary transaction costs and tax implications, while rebalancing too infrequently can result in your portfolio drifting too far from your target allocation.

1. Annual Rebalancing

Rebalancing your portfolio once a year is a common approach that strikes a balance between maintaining alignment with your target allocation and minimizing transaction costs. Annual rebalancing allows you to review your portfolio's performance over the past year and make adjustments as needed.
- Advantages:
- Simplicity: Annual rebalancing is easy to implement and requires minimal monitoring throughout the year.
- Cost Efficiency: Rebalancing once a year helps reduce transaction costs and tax implications, particularly for long-term investors.
- Considerations:
- Potential for Drift: Depending on market conditions, your portfolio may drift significantly from your target allocation within a year, potentially increasing your risk exposure.
- Application:
If you prefer a straightforward and low-maintenance approach, annual rebalancing may be the right choice. Schedule your annual rebalancing at a time that aligns with your financial planning, such as the beginning of the year or after your annual portfolio review.

2. Semi-Annual or Quarterly Rebalancing

Rebalancing your portfolio semi-annually or quarterly provides more frequent adjustments, helping you stay closer to your target allocation throughout the year. This approach is particularly useful during periods of market volatility when asset prices may fluctuate more rapidly.
- Advantages:
- Better Alignment: More frequent rebalancing helps you maintain a closer alignment with your target allocation, reducing the risk of significant drift.
- Responsive to Market Changes: Semi-annual or quarterly rebalancing allows you to respond more quickly to market movements, potentially reducing risk.
- Considerations:

- Higher Costs: More frequent rebalancing can lead to increased transaction costs, particularly if your portfolio includes individual stocks or ETFs with trading fees.

- Increased Time Commitment: Semi-annual or quarterly rebalancing requires more frequent monitoring and adjustments, which can be time-consuming.

- Application: If you're comfortable with a more hands-on approach and want to maintain closer control over your portfolio, semi-annual or quarterly rebalancing may be appropriate. Monitor your portfolio regularly and set reminders to review and rebalance every six months or three months.

3. Event-Driven Rebalancing

Event-driven rebalancing involves adjusting your portfolio in response to specific events, such as significant market movements, changes in your financial situation, or major life events. This approach is less about adhering to a fixed schedule and more about being responsive to important developments.

- Advantages:

- Tailored Adjustments: Event-driven rebalancing allows you to make adjustments based on specific circumstances that may impact your portfolio, ensuring that your allocation remains relevant to your current situation.

- Flexibility: This method provides the flexibility to rebalance only when necessary, potentially reducing transaction costs and avoiding unnecessary trades.

- Considerations:

- Potential for Infrequent Rebalancing: If no significant events occur, your portfolio may go unbalanced for an extended period, leading to potential drift.

- Requires Vigilance: Event-driven rebalancing requires you to stay vigilant and be aware of any events that may warrant a portfolio adjustment.

- Application: Event-driven rebalancing is ideal for investors who prefer a flexible approach and are confident in their ability to monitor their portfolio and react to changes. Use this method in combination with a regular review schedule to ensure that your portfolio remains aligned with your goals.

Conclusion: Crafting Your Rebalancing Strategy

Rebalancing is an essential component of portfolio management that helps you maintain control over your investments, manage risk, and stay aligned with your financial goals. By understanding the importance of rebalancing, exploring different rebalancing methods, and determining the right frequency for your situation, you can develop a strategy that supports your long-term success.

As a Minimalistic Entrepreneur, the discipline of regular rebalancing is key to building a resilient and diversified portfolio. Whether you choose a calendar-based, threshold-based, or event-driven approach, the goal is to stay true to your investment strategy while adapting to changing market conditions and personal circumstances.

Remember, rebalancing is not just about maintaining a specific asset allocation—it's about staying proactive, disciplined, and focused on your long-term objectives. By incorporating rebalancing into your regular portfolio management routine, you'll be better equipped to navigate the ups and downs of the market and continue on your path to financial independence.

CHAPTER TEN

THE MINIMALISTIC ENTREPRENEUR LIFESTYLE

Achieving Financial Freedom Through Passive Income

Financial freedom is the ultimate goal for many aspiring entrepreneurs and investors. It represents a state of financial independence where your passive income—money earned with little to no effort—exceeds your living expenses. Achieving this level of financial autonomy allows you to live life on your terms, free from the constraints of a traditional 9-to-5 job. As a Minimalistic Entrepreneur, financial freedom is not just about accumulating wealth but about creating a sustainable lifestyle that supports your goals, passions, and personal well-being.

In this chapter, we'll explore what financial freedom truly means, how to calculate your passive income needs, and the strategies you can employ to increase your passive income over time. By the end of this chapter, you'll have a clear roadmap to achieving financial freedom through passive income, empowering you to design the life you've always envisioned.

Defining Financial Freedom: What Does It Really Mean?

Financial freedom is often defined as having enough passive income to cover your living expenses, allowing you to maintain your desired lifestyle without relying on active employment. However, financial freedom is more than just a number—it's a mindset and a lifestyle choice that prioritizes autonomy, flexibility, and purpose.

1. The Essence of Financial Freedom

At its core, financial freedom is about choice. It's the ability to decide how you spend your time, pursue your passions, and live according to your values without being constrained by financial limitations. When you achieve financial freedom, you gain the power to:

- Pursue Your Passions: With financial freedom, you can focus on activities that bring you joy and fulfillment, whether that's starting a business, traveling the world, or dedicating time to hobbies and creative pursuits.

- Live Without Financial Stress: Achieving financial freedom means you no longer have to worry about making ends meet or living paycheck to paycheck. You have a financial cushion that provides peace of mind and security.

- Create a Flexible Lifestyle: Financial freedom allows you to design a lifestyle that aligns with your personal values and priorities. Whether you prefer a minimalist lifestyle with fewer material possessions or a more luxurious one, financial freedom gives you the flexibility to choose.

- Make Impactful Decisions: With financial freedom, you have the resources to make decisions that align with your long-term goals and values, such as supporting causes you care about or investing in opportunities that contribute to a better world.

2. The Financial Independence, Retire Early (FIRE) Movement

The concept of financial freedom is closely associated with the Financial Independence, Retire Early (FIRE) movement. FIRE advocates emphasize the importance of saving aggressively, investing wisely, and living frugally to achieve financial independence at a younger age. While not everyone aspires to retire early, the principles of the FIRE movement—such as prioritizing savings and maximizing passive income—are valuable for anyone seeking financial freedom.

3. Tailoring Financial Freedom to Your Lifestyle

Financial freedom looks different for everyone, depending on their lifestyle, values, and goals. Some may aim for a modest level of financial freedom that covers basic living expenses, while others may seek a higher level of freedom that allows for more luxurious or expansive pursuits.

- Application: Reflect on what financial freedom means to you personally. Consider your ideal lifestyle, your passions, and your long-term goals. Define what financial freedom looks like in your context, and use this definition as a guiding star in your journey toward independence.

Calculating Your Passive Income Needs: How Much Is Enough?

To achieve financial freedom, you need to determine how much passive income you'll need to cover your living expenses and sustain your desired lifestyle. This calculation is a crucial step in setting realistic financial goals and creating a plan to reach them.

1. Assessing Your Living Expenses

The first step in calculating your passive income needs is to assess your current living expenses. This includes both essential expenses (such as housing, utilities, groceries, and healthcare) and discretionary spending (such as entertainment, travel, and dining out).

- Application: Track your monthly expenses over a period of several months to get an accurate picture of your spending habits. Categorize your expenses into essential and discretionary categories to understand where your money is going.

2. Estimating Future Expenses

Your future expenses may differ from your current ones, depending on factors such as inflation, lifestyle changes, or new financial goals. Consider how your expenses might change over time and adjust your calculations accordingly.

- Application: Account for potential changes in your living expenses, such as increased healthcare costs as you age, higher travel expenses if you plan to travel frequently, or reduced expenses if you downsize your home or adopt a more minimalist lifestyle.

3. Setting a Target Passive Income Goal

Once you have a clear understanding of your current and future expenses, you can set a target passive income goal. This is the amount of passive income you need to generate each month (or year) to cover your expenses and achieve financial freedom.

- Application: Multiply your monthly living expenses by 12 to calculate your annual expenses. Add a buffer (e.g., 10-20%) to account for unexpected costs or emergencies. This gives you your annual passive income target. For example, if your annual expenses are ₹12,00,000, you might set a target of ₹13,20,000 to ensure you have a safety net.

4. The 4% Rule

The 4% rule is a commonly used guideline for determining how much you need to have invested to achieve financial independence. It's based on the idea that you can withdraw 4% of your investment portfolio each year without depleting your principal, assuming your investments continue to grow.

- Application: Divide your annual passive income target by 4% (or multiply by 25) to calculate the size of the investment portfolio you need to achieve financial freedom. For example, if your target is ₹13,20,000 per year, you would need a portfolio of ₹3,30,00,000 (₹13,20,000 ÷ 0.04) to generate that income.

5. Adjusting for Personal Factors

The 4% rule is a general guideline, but your actual withdrawal rate may vary based on factors such as your risk tolerance, investment strategy, and life expectancy. Adjust your calculations to reflect your personal circumstances and financial goals.

- Application: If you prefer a more conservative approach, you might use a lower withdrawal rate (e.g., 3%) to ensure your portfolio lasts longer. Alternatively, if you're willing to take on more risk, you might use a higher withdrawal rate (e.g., 5%) with the understanding that your portfolio may fluctuate more over time.

Strategies to Increase Passive Income Over Time: Building Your Financial Freedom

Achieving financial freedom requires not only reaching your passive income target but also continuously growing your income to stay ahead of inflation and support your evolving lifestyle. There are several strategies you can use to increase your passive income over time.

1. Dividend Investing

Dividend investing involves purchasing stocks that pay regular dividends, providing a steady stream of income. Dividend stocks are often issued by established companies with a history of profitability and stable cash flow. Reinvesting dividends can also lead to compounding growth, further increasing your income over time.

- Application: Build a portfolio of dividend-paying stocks, focusing on companies with a track record of consistent dividend payments and growth. Consider using a dividend reinvestment plan (DRIP) to automatically reinvest your dividends and compound your returns.

2. Real Estate Investing

Real estate is a popular avenue for generating passive income through rental properties, real estate investment trusts (REITs), or crowdfunding platforms. Rental properties can provide a steady income stream, while REITs offer a more hands-off approach to real estate investing.

- Application: Consider investing in rental properties that generate positive cash flow, or diversify your portfolio with REITs that pay regular dividends. Evaluate the potential for property appreciation and rental income growth when selecting real estate investments.

3. Peer-to-Peer Lending

Peer-to-peer (P2P) lending platforms allow you to lend money directly to individuals or small businesses in exchange for interest payments. This can be a way to generate passive income while diversifying your investment portfolio.

- Application: Explore reputable P2P lending platforms and diversify your loans across multiple borrowers to reduce risk. Be aware of the potential for default and consider the interest rates offered to ensure they align with your risk tolerance.

4. Royalties from Intellectual Property

If you have creative talents, you can generate passive income through royalties from intellectual property, such as books, music, art, or patents. Royalties provide ongoing income whenever your work is used or sold.

- Application: Focus on creating intellectual property that has long-term value and appeal. Collaborate with publishers, production companies, or licensing agencies to distribute your work and collect royalties over time.

5. Investing in Bonds and Fixed-Income Securities

Bonds and fixed-income securities offer a stable source of passive income through interest payments. While they may not offer the same growth potential as stocks, they provide a reliable income stream, particularly for conservative investors.

- Application: Diversify your portfolio with high-quality bonds, such as government or corporate bonds, to generate regular interest income. Consider laddering your bond investments to manage interest rate risk and ensure a steady income stream over time.

6. Building a Diverse Income Stream

Diversification is key to increasing your passive income and reducing risk. By building multiple streams of income across different asset classes and investment types, you can create a more resilient financial foundation that can weather economic downturns and market fluctuations.

- Application: Aim to build a portfolio that includes a mix of dividend-paying stocks, real estate, bonds, digital products, and other passive income sources. Regularly review and adjust your income streams to ensure they align with your financial goals and risk tolerance.

Conclusion: The Path to Financial Freedom

Achieving financial freedom through passive income is a journey that requires careful planning, disciplined execution, and a long-term perspective. By defining what financial freedom means to you, calculating your passive income needs, and implementing strategies to grow your income over time, you can create a lifestyle that aligns with your values, passions, and personal goals.

As a Minimalistic Entrepreneur, financial freedom is not just about accumulating wealth—it's about creating a life of purpose, fulfillment, and autonomy. By focusing on passive income, you can free yourself from the constraints of traditional employment and design a lifestyle that allows you to pursue your dreams, make a positive impact, and live on your own terms.

Remember, the journey to financial freedom is a marathon, not a sprint. Stay committed to your goals, be patient in your investments, and continuously seek opportunities to increase your passive income. With dedication and perseverance, financial freedom is within your reach, empowering you to live the life you've always imagined.

Balancing Minimalistic Entrepreneurship with Other Pursuits

One of the core principles of minimalistic entrepreneurship is the belief that life is about more than just work and accumulating wealth. It's about creating a balanced, fulfilling life that allows you to pursue your passions, hobbies, and personal growth alongside your entrepreneurial and investment endeavors. Achieving this balance requires careful time management, a commitment to your personal interests, and a dedication to continuous learning and self-improvement.

In this part, we'll explore how to effectively manage your time as a passive investor, how to integrate your passions and hobbies into your daily life, and the importance of continuous learning and personal growth. By the end of this chapter, you'll have a clear understanding of how to create a harmonious lifestyle that supports both your financial goals and your broader aspirations.

Time Management for Passive Investors: Maximizing Efficiency, Minimizing Stress

As a minimalistic entrepreneur focused on passive income, effective time management is crucial. The goal is to maximize the efficiency of your investment activities, freeing up time for other pursuits that bring joy and fulfillment. By implementing smart time management strategies, you can ensure that your financial goals are met without sacrificing the other aspects of your life.

1. Automate Where Possible

Automation is one of the most powerful tools for managing your time as a passive investor. By automating routine tasks, you can reduce the time spent on managing your investments and focus on higher-value activities.

- Investment Automation: Use automatic investment plans, such as systematic investment plans (SIPs) or dividend reinvestment plans (DRIPs), to regularly invest without manual intervention. Automating your investments ensures consistency and takes advantage of dollar-cost averaging.

- Bill Payments and Savings: Set up automatic bill payments and savings transfers to ensure that your financial obligations are met without the need for constant oversight. This also includes automating contributions to retirement accounts or other long-term savings goals.

- Monitoring and Alerts: Leverage portfolio management tools that provide automated alerts and reports. These tools can notify you of significant changes in your portfolio, helping you stay informed without needing to monitor the market daily.

2. Prioritize High-Impact Activities

Not all investment activities are created equal. Focus on high-impact activities that contribute most significantly to your financial goals, and minimize time spent on tasks that offer little return.

- Portfolio Reviews: Schedule regular portfolio reviews, such as quarterly or semi-annual check-ins, to assess performance and make necessary adjustments. During these reviews, focus on key performance indicators (KPIs) and rebalancing needs rather than getting bogged down in daily market movements.

- Learning and Research: Dedicate time to learning about new investment opportunities, trends, and strategies that can enhance your portfolio. Prioritize research that has the potential to significantly impact your investment outcomes, such as exploring new asset classes or sectors.

- Delegation: If you find certain investment tasks time-consuming or outside your expertise, consider delegating them to a financial advisor or using robo-advisors. This allows you to focus on areas where you add the most value, whether that's strategic decision-making or pursuing other interests.

3. Set Boundaries for Work and Play

Balancing minimalistic entrepreneurship with other pursuits requires clear boundaries between your investment activities and personal time. Establishing these boundaries helps you avoid burnout and ensures that you dedicate time to the things that matter most outside of work.

- Time Blocking: Use time blocking to allocate specific periods of your day or week to investment-related activities. For example, you might reserve an hour every Sunday morning for portfolio reviews and research, while leaving the rest of the day free for family, hobbies, or relaxation.

- Disconnecting from Work: Make it a habit to disconnect from investment activities during certain times, such as evenings or weekends. This allows you to fully engage in other pursuits without the distraction of market fluctuations or financial news.

- Mindfulness and Reflection: Incorporate mindfulness practices, such as meditation or journaling, into your routine to reflect on your priorities and ensure that your time is aligned with your values. This practice can help you stay grounded and focused on what truly matters.

Pursuing Passions and Hobbies: Enriching Your Life Beyond Finance

A fulfilling life is not just about financial success; it's also about pursuing passions and hobbies that bring joy, creativity, and meaning to your everyday experiences. As a minimalistic entrepreneur, it's important to make time for these activities, even as you work toward your financial goals.

1. Identifying Your Passions

Start by identifying the activities that genuinely excite and inspire you. These might be creative pursuits, physical activities, or intellectual challenges that provide a sense of fulfillment and personal growth.

- Reflection: Take time to reflect on the activities that bring you the most joy and satisfaction. Consider the hobbies you enjoyed in the past, the things you've always wanted to try, or the activities that make you lose track of time.

- Exploration: If you're unsure of your passions, explore different hobbies and interests to see what resonates with you. This could include taking up a new sport, learning a musical instrument, or diving into a new area of study.

2. Integrating Passions into Your Routine

Once you've identified your passions, the next step is to integrate them into your daily or weekly routine. Balancing work with personal pursuits requires intentional effort, but the rewards are well worth it.

- Scheduling Time for Hobbies: Just as you schedule time for work and financial planning, schedule regular time for your hobbies and passions. Whether it's a weekly painting class, a daily run, or a weekend hike, making time for these activities ensures they become a consistent part of your life.

- Combining Passions with Social Connections: Many hobbies offer opportunities to connect with like-minded individuals, which can enhance your enjoyment and motivation. Consider joining clubs, groups, or communities centered around your interests, whether that's a book club, a local sports team, or an online forum for hobbyists.

- Balancing Multiple Interests: If you have multiple passions, find ways to balance them without feeling overwhelmed. You might dedicate certain days of the week to different activities or rotate through your hobbies on a seasonal basis, allowing you to fully immerse yourself in each one.

3. The Role of Passion in Personal Fulfillment

Pursuing your passions is not just about having fun; it's also about personal fulfillment and mental well-being. Engaging in activities you love can reduce stress, boost creativity, and provide a sense of purpose that complements your entrepreneurial pursuits.

- Mental Health and Well-Being: Hobbies and passions play a crucial role in maintaining mental health. They provide an outlet for stress relief, relaxation, and creative expression, which are essential for a balanced life.

- Creative Problem-Solving: Engaging in creative or intellectual pursuits outside of work can enhance your problem-solving skills in your entrepreneurial endeavors. The fresh perspectives and ideas you gain from hobbies can often be applied to your business and investment strategies.

- Life Satisfaction: Ultimately, pursuing your passions contributes to a greater sense of life satisfaction. It allows you to live a more well-rounded life, where success is not just measured by financial achievements but by the richness of your experiences.

Continuous Learning and Personal Growth: Evolving as a Minimalistic Entrepreneur

In a rapidly changing world, continuous learning and personal growth are essential for staying relevant, adaptable, and fulfilled. As a minimalistic entrepreneur, committing to lifelong learning helps you refine your skills, expand your knowledge, and stay ahead in both your financial and personal life.

1. Embracing Lifelong Learning

Lifelong learning is the practice of continually acquiring new knowledge and skills throughout your life. It's about staying curious, open-minded, and willing to adapt to new challenges and opportunities.

- Formal Education: Consider enrolling in courses, workshops, or certification programs that align with your interests and goals. This could include financial courses to enhance your investment knowledge, or creative workshops to develop new skills.

- Informal Learning: Lifelong learning doesn't have to be formal. It can also include reading books, listening to podcasts, attending seminars, or engaging in discussions with experts and peers. The key is to remain curious and open to new ideas.

- Learning from Experiences: Every experience, whether positive or negative, offers an opportunity for growth. Reflect on your successes and challenges, and use them as learning tools to improve your approach and decision-making in the future.

2. Fostering a Growth Mindset

A growth mindset is the belief that your abilities and intelligence can be developed through effort, learning, and persistence. Embracing a growth mindset allows you to approach challenges with resilience and view failures as opportunities for improvement.

- Challenges as Opportunities: Instead of avoiding challenges, embrace them as opportunities to learn and grow. Whether it's tackling a difficult project, learning a new skill, or stepping out of your comfort zone, a growth mindset encourages continuous improvement.

- Resilience in the Face of Setbacks: View setbacks and failures as part of the learning process. Reflect on what went wrong, extract valuable lessons, and apply them to future endeavors. Resilience is key to long-term success and personal growth.

- Celebrating Progress: Recognize and celebrate your progress, no matter how small. Acknowledging your achievements and growth reinforces your commitment to learning and motivates you to keep pushing forward.

3. Integrating Learning into Daily Life

Continuous learning doesn't have to be time-consuming or overwhelming. By integrating learning into your daily life, you can make steady progress without sacrificing other pursuits.

- Daily Learning Rituals: Incorporate small learning rituals into your daily routine, such as reading for 20 minutes each morning, listening to an educational podcast during your commute, or setting aside time for reflection and journaling at the end of the day.

- Experimentation and Practice: Apply what you learn in real-life situations. Whether it's testing a new investment strategy, experimenting with a creative project, or practicing a new skill, hands-on experience is one of the most effective ways to reinforce learning.

- Connecting with Mentors and Peers: Engage with mentors, peers, and like-minded individuals who can offer guidance, support, and new perspectives. Learning from others' experiences and insights can accelerate your own growth and open doors to new opportunities.

Conclusion: Crafting a Balanced and Fulfilling Life

Balancing minimalistic entrepreneurship with other pursuits is about creating a life that is rich in experiences, passions, and personal growth. By managing your time effectively, pursuing the activities that bring you joy, and committing to continuous learning, you can design a lifestyle that supports both your financial goals and your broader aspirations.

As a Minimalistic Entrepreneur, your journey is not just about building wealth—it's about living a life of purpose, fulfillment, and balance. By integrating your passions, hobbies, and learning into your daily routine, you can achieve a harmonious lifestyle that allows you to thrive both personally and professionally.

Remember, life is about more than just work and financial success. It's about exploring your passions, nurturing your well-being, and constantly growing as an individual. By embracing these principles, you'll not only achieve financial freedom but also create a life that is truly worth living.

Scaling Your Investments Over Time

Building wealth through minimalistic entrepreneurship is not just about getting started with investments—it's about scaling those investments over time to achieve financial freedom and beyond. Scaling involves consistently growing your portfolio by reinvesting earnings, increasing your investment contributions, and exploring new opportunities that align with your financial goals and risk tolerance.

In this Part, we'll delve into the strategies for scaling your investments effectively. We'll cover the importance of reinvesting dividends and capital gains, the benefits of increasing your investment contributions, and how to explore new investment opportunities as you advance in your financial journey. By the end of this chapter, you'll have a clear plan for scaling your investments, allowing you to maximize returns and accelerate your path to financial independence.

Reinvesting Dividends and Capital Gains: The Power of Compounding

One of the most powerful tools for scaling your investments is the reinvestment of dividends and capital gains. Reinvestment leverages the principle of compounding, where the returns on your investments generate additional returns, leading to exponential growth over time.

1. Understanding the Impact of Reinvestment

When you reinvest dividends and capital gains, you're essentially using the income generated by your investments to purchase more shares of the same stock, fund, or asset. This not only increases your overall investment in the asset but also amplifies your future returns, as the additional shares themselves start generating dividends and gains.

- Compounding Effect: The true power of reinvestment lies in compounding. As your reinvested dividends and gains generate their own returns, your portfolio grows at an accelerating rate. Over the long term, this can significantly enhance your wealth and bring you closer to your financial goals faster.

- Application: Set up automatic dividend reinvestment plans (DRIPs) through your brokerage account. This allows dividends to be reinvested immediately, ensuring that your money is consistently working for you. For mutual funds and ETFs, you can usually elect to reinvest capital gains automatically, contributing to the compounding effect.

2. Dividend Reinvestment Strategies

Different strategies for reinvesting dividends can help you optimize returns based on your investment goals and risk tolerance.

- Reinvesting in the Same Asset: The simplest strategy is to reinvest dividends directly into the same stock or fund that generated them. This is particularly effective for high-quality, dividend-paying stocks with strong growth potential, as it allows you to accumulate more shares over time.

- Diversifying with Reinvested Dividends: Another strategy is to reinvest dividends into different assets to enhance diversification. For example, you might reinvest dividends from a stock fund into a bond fund, balancing your portfolio and managing risk.

- Application: Choose a reinvestment strategy that aligns with your long-term goals. If you're focused on growth, reinvesting dividends into high-growth assets may be the best option. If you're nearing retirement or have a lower risk tolerance, diversifying your reinvested dividends can help create a more balanced portfolio.

3. Reinvesting Capital Gains

Capital gains are the profits you realize when you sell an investment for more than you paid for it. Reinvesting these gains can further accelerate your portfolio's growth, especially if done strategically.

- Timing and Tax Considerations: When reinvesting capital gains, it's important to consider the timing of your sales and the associated tax implications. In many countries, long-term capital gains (from assets held for more than a year) are taxed at a lower rate than short-term gains, so timing your sales to qualify for long-term gains can be advantageous.

- Targeting High-Growth Opportunities: Reinvesting capital gains into high-growth opportunities can amplify your returns. Look for emerging industries, innovative companies, or undervalued assets that have strong growth potential.

- Application: After realizing a capital gain, reinvest the proceeds in assets that align with your risk tolerance and financial goals. If you're focused on growth, consider reinvesting in sectors or companies with high upside potential. If you're risk-averse, reinvest in more stable, income-generating assets.

Increasing Investment Contributions: Accelerating Your Path to Wealth

Another key strategy for scaling your investments is to increase your contributions over time. As your income grows, dedicating a larger portion of it to investments can significantly boost your portfolio's value and expedite your journey to financial freedom.

1. The Power of Incremental Increases

Small, incremental increases in your investment contributions can have a substantial impact over time. By regularly increasing the amount you invest, you can accelerate the growth of your portfolio without making drastic changes to your lifestyle.

- Annual Contribution Increases: Consider increasing your investment contributions each year, even if it's by a small percentage. For example, if you're currently investing ₹10,000 per month, you might increase that amount to ₹11,000 next year, ₹12,000 the following year, and so on. These incremental increases compound over time, leading to significant portfolio growth.

- Application: Set a goal to increase your investment contributions annually, or whenever you receive a raise or bonus. Automate these contributions to ensure consistency, and review your budget regularly to identify opportunities to allocate more towards investments.

2. Leveraging Salary Increases and Bonuses

As your career progresses and your income increases, you have an opportunity to allocate more towards your investments. Instead of letting lifestyle inflation consume your additional income, direct a significant portion of salary increases, bonuses, or windfalls into your investment accounts.

- Avoiding Lifestyle Inflation: Lifestyle inflation occurs when your spending increases in proportion to your income. By consciously directing salary increases and bonuses into investments, you can avoid this pitfall and ensure that your wealth grows faster than your expenses.

- Application: Commit to investing a portion of every salary increase or bonus you receive. For example, you might choose to invest 50% of any salary increase and 100% of any bonuses. This approach allows you to enjoy some of the additional income while still prioritizing your long-term financial goals.

3. Maximizing Retirement Contributions

Retirement accounts, such as a 401(k), IRA, or the Indian Public Provident Fund (PPF), offer tax advantages that can enhance your investment returns. Maximizing contributions to these accounts not only helps you build a substantial retirement nest egg but also provides immediate tax benefits.

- Taking Advantage of Employer Matches: If your employer offers a matching contribution to your retirement account, take full advantage of it. Employer matches are essentially free money that can significantly boost your retirement savings.

- Application: Aim to contribute the maximum allowed amount to your retirement accounts each year. If you're not currently maxing out your contributions, gradually increase them until you reach the limit. Prioritize contributions to accounts with employer matches to maximize the benefit.

Exploring New Investment Opportunities: Expanding Your Horizons

As your investment portfolio grows, exploring new opportunities can help you diversify, enhance returns, and stay ahead of market trends. Diversification is key to managing risk, while strategic allocation to emerging opportunities can provide significant upside potential.

1. Diversifying Across Asset Classes

Diversification across different asset classes—such as stocks, bonds, real estate, and commodities—can help manage risk and reduce the impact of market volatility on your portfolio. Each asset class responds differently to economic conditions, so spreading your investments across multiple classes can create a more resilient portfolio.

- Exploring Alternative Investments: In addition to traditional asset classes, consider exploring alternative investments such as private equity, hedge funds, or cryptocurrencies. While these can be riskier, they also offer the potential for higher returns and can be a valuable addition to a diversified portfolio.

- Application: Review your current portfolio to identify areas where diversification could be improved. Consider adding new asset classes or increasing exposure to underrepresented sectors. If you're considering alternative investments, start with a small allocation and increase it gradually as you become more comfortable.

2. Investing in Emerging Markets

Emerging markets, such as India, China, Brazil, and Southeast Asia, offer significant growth potential due to their expanding economies and rising middle classes. Investing in these markets can provide exposure to industries and companies that are poised for rapid growth.

- Risks and Rewards: While emerging markets can offer high returns, they also come with higher risks, including political instability, currency fluctuations, and less mature regulatory environments. Balancing the potential rewards with these risks is crucial when investing in emerging markets.

- Application: Consider allocating a portion of your portfolio to emerging markets, either through individual stocks, mutual funds, or ETFs. Focus on sectors that are expected to drive growth, such as technology, consumer goods, and infrastructure.

3. Keeping Up with Technological Innovations

Technological innovation is a major driver of growth in today's economy. Investing in companies at the forefront of innovation—such as those involved in artificial intelligence, biotechnology, renewable energy, and fintech—can provide significant long-term returns.

- Identifying Innovators: Look for companies that are leaders in their fields, have strong research and development (R&D) capabilities, and are positioned to benefit from emerging technologies. Consider also investing in technology-focused ETFs that provide broad exposure to the sector.

- Application: Allocate a portion of your portfolio to technology stocks or funds that focus on innovative companies. Stay informed about technological trends and adjust your investments as new opportunities arise.

4. Expanding into Real Estate and REITs

Real estate is a time-tested asset class that offers the potential for both income and capital appreciation. If you're looking to diversify your portfolio and generate passive income, real estate investments—whether through direct property ownership or real estate investment trusts (REITs)—can be a valuable addition.

- Direct Ownership vs. REITs: Direct property ownership involves purchasing and managing physical properties, which can provide steady rental income and

potential appreciation. REITs, on the other hand, allow you to invest in real estate without the responsibilities of property management, offering liquidity and diversification.

- Application: Evaluate your financial goals and risk tolerance to determine whether direct ownership or REITs are a better fit. If you're interested in direct ownership, start by researching local real estate markets and identifying properties with strong cash flow potential. If you prefer a more hands-off approach, consider adding REITs to your portfolio for exposure to real estate without the need for active management.

Conclusion: Scaling for Sustained Growth

Scaling your investments over time is a critical component of achieving and maintaining financial freedom. By reinvesting dividends and capital gains, increasing your investment contributions, and exploring new opportunities, you can grow your wealth and create a more resilient, diversified portfolio.

As a Minimalistic Entrepreneur, the journey to financial independence is not just about making smart investments—it's about continuously evolving your strategy to adapt to changing market conditions, new opportunities, and your own personal goals. By staying committed to scaling your investments and being open to new ideas, you can build a financial foundation that supports a life of freedom, fulfillment, and lasting success.

Remember, scaling your investments is a long-term endeavor. It requires patience, discipline, and a willingness to learn and adapt. But with the right approach, you can achieve exponential growth, turning your financial aspirations into reality and creating a legacy that endures for generations.

CHAPTER ELEVEN

THE FUTURE OF MINIMALISTIC ENTREPRENEURSHIP

Emerging Trends in Stock Market Investing

As a Minimalistic Entrepreneur, staying ahead of emerging trends in stock market investing is crucial to ensuring that your investment strategies remain relevant and effective in a rapidly changing world. The landscape of investing is continuously evolving, driven by advancements in technology, shifts in societal values, and changes in the global economy. By understanding these trends and adapting your approach, you can position yourself to capitalize on new opportunities while mitigating potential risks.

In this part, we will explore three significant trends shaping the future of stock market investing: the rise of ESG (Environmental, Social, Governance) investing, the impact of artificial intelligence and big data, and the changing global economic landscapes. By the end of this chapter, you will have a deeper understanding of these trends and how they can influence your investment decisions, allowing you to remain agile and informed in your pursuit of financial freedom.

The Rise of ESG (Environmental, Social, Governance) Investing: Aligning Values with Profits

In recent years, ESG investing has gained significant traction among investors who are increasingly prioritizing sustainability and ethical considerations alongside financial returns. ESG investing involves evaluating companies based on their performance in three key areas: environmental stewardship, social responsibility, and governance practices. This approach reflects a broader shift toward conscious capitalism, where investors seek to align their portfolios with their personal values while still achieving competitive returns.

1. Understanding ESG Criteria

ESG criteria provide a framework for assessing a company's long-term sustainability and ethical impact. These criteria are divided into three main categories:

- Environmental (E): This criterion evaluates a company's environmental impact, including its efforts to reduce carbon emissions, manage waste, conserve natural resources, and promote renewable energy. Companies with strong environmental practices are often seen as better equipped to navigate regulatory changes and respond to growing consumer demand for sustainability.

- Social (S): Social criteria examine how a company manages relationships with its employees, customers, suppliers, and communities. This includes issues such as labor practices, diversity and inclusion, human rights, and community engagement. Companies that prioritize social responsibility tend to build stronger brands and foster loyalty among stakeholders.

- Governance (G): Governance criteria assess a company's leadership, board composition, executive compensation, transparency, and shareholder rights. Strong governance practices are essential for ensuring accountability, reducing risks of fraud or misconduct, and promoting long-term value creation.

2. The Financial Performance of ESG Investments

One of the key considerations for investors is whether ESG investing can deliver competitive financial returns. While ESG-focused companies are often associated with lower risk due to their emphasis on sustainability and ethical practices, they also have the potential for strong financial performance.

- Risk Mitigation: Companies that excel in ESG criteria are typically better at managing risks related to environmental regulations, social controversies, and governance failures. This can lead to more stable financial performance and reduced volatility in the long term.

- Market Outperformance: Studies have shown that ESG-focused companies can outperform their peers over time, particularly in sectors where sustainability is becoming increasingly important. For example, companies in the renewable energy sector or those with strong diversity initiatives may see higher growth rates as societal values shift.

- Application: Consider integrating ESG criteria into your investment strategy by selecting companies or funds that score highly on ESG metrics. You can use ESG ratings provided by financial data providers or invest in ESG-focused ETFs and mutual funds that align with your values.

3. The Growing Popularity of Impact Investing

Impact investing, a subset of ESG investing, goes a step further by focusing on investments that generate measurable social or environmental benefits alongside financial returns. Impact investors seek to address global challenges such as climate change, poverty, and inequality through their investment choices.

- Social Impact: Impact investments aim to create positive social outcomes, such as improving access to education, healthcare, and affordable housing. These investments often target underserved communities or regions and seek to address systemic issues.

- Environmental Impact: Environmental impact investments focus on combating climate change, promoting clean energy, and preserving natural resources. This includes investments in renewable energy projects, sustainable agriculture, and conservation efforts.

- Application: If you're passionate about making a difference through your investments, explore impact investing opportunities. Look for funds or companies that have a clear mission to drive positive change, and consider how these investments fit into your broader portfolio.

The Impact of Artificial Intelligence and Big Data: Transforming Investment Strategies

Artificial intelligence (AI) and big data are revolutionizing the world of stock market investing, providing investors with unprecedented insights and predictive capabilities. These technologies are enabling more sophisticated analysis, personalized investment strategies, and faster decision-making, all of which can enhance the effectiveness of your investment approach.

1. AI-Powered Investment Analysis

Artificial intelligence has the potential to transform how investors analyze stocks and make decisions. By processing vast amounts of data at high speeds, AI can identify patterns, trends, and correlations that may be missed by human analysts.

- Predictive Analytics: AI algorithms can analyze historical data, market trends, and economic indicators to predict future stock movements and market conditions. This allows investors to make more informed decisions and potentially capitalize on emerging opportunities.

- Sentiment Analysis: AI can also analyze sentiment from news articles, social media, and other sources to gauge market sentiment and investor behavior. This can provide valuable insights into market psychology and help investors anticipate market reactions.

- Application: Consider incorporating AI-powered tools and platforms into your investment strategy. These tools can provide data-driven insights, automate routine tasks, and enhance your ability to identify profitable opportunities in the market.

2. Big Data and Personalized Investment Strategies

Big data refers to the vast amounts of structured and unstructured data generated from various sources, including financial transactions, social media activity, and consumer behavior. Analyzing big data can provide deeper insights into market trends, consumer preferences, and economic conditions, allowing for more personalized and effective investment strategies.

- Customizing Portfolios: Big data enables the creation of highly personalized investment portfolios tailored to an individual's risk tolerance, financial goals, and preferences. By analyzing data on investor behavior, preferences, and market conditions, AI-powered platforms can design portfolios that are optimized for each investor's unique needs.

- Real-Time Market Analysis: Big data allows for real-time analysis of market conditions, providing investors with up-to-the-minute insights that can inform trading decisions. This level of analysis can be particularly valuable in fast-moving markets where timely decisions are critical.

- Application: Explore investment platforms that leverage big data to offer personalized portfolio recommendations and real-time market analysis. These platforms can help you make more informed decisions and optimize your investment strategy for better outcomes.

3. The Role of Robo-Advisors

Robo-advisors are AI-driven platforms that provide automated investment management services. These platforms use algorithms to create and manage investment portfolios based on an individual's risk tolerance, financial goals, and preferences. Robo-advisors have democratized access to sophisticated investment strategies, making them available to a broader audience.

- Cost Efficiency: Robo-advisors typically offer lower fees compared to traditional financial advisors, making them an attractive option for investors seeking cost-effective portfolio management.

- Automated Rebalancing: Many robo-advisors offer automated rebalancing, ensuring that your portfolio remains aligned with your target asset allocation. This helps maintain your desired risk level and optimize returns over time.

- Application: Consider using a robo-advisor if you're looking for a hands-off, cost-effective way to manage your investments. Robo-advisors can be particularly useful for investors who prefer a set-it-and-forget-it approach, allowing you to focus on other aspects of your life while your portfolio is managed by advanced algorithms.

Changing Global Economic Landscapes: Adapting to a New World Order

The global economic landscape is undergoing significant shifts, driven by factors such as geopolitical developments, technological advancements, and changing demographics. These changes are reshaping the investment environment, presenting both challenges and opportunities for investors.

1. The Rise of Emerging Markets

Emerging markets, including countries in Asia, Latin America, and Africa, are becoming increasingly important players in the global economy. These regions offer significant growth potential due to their expanding middle classes, youthful populations, and ongoing urbanization.

- Growth Potential: Emerging markets are expected to drive a substantial portion of global economic growth in the coming decades. Investors who allocate a portion of their portfolios to these markets can benefit from the rapid expansion of industries such as technology, consumer goods, and infrastructure.

- Risks and Considerations: While emerging markets offer high growth potential, they also come with higher risks, including political instability, currency fluctuations, and less mature regulatory environments. It's important to balance the potential rewards with these risks when investing in emerging markets.

- Application: Diversify your portfolio by including exposure to emerging markets. Consider using ETFs or mutual funds that focus on these regions, and stay informed about geopolitical developments that may impact your investments.

2. The Impact of Globalization and Trade

Globalization has transformed the way businesses operate, creating interconnected supply chains and expanding access to international markets. However, the rise of protectionism and trade tensions in recent years has introduced new challenges and uncertainties for global investors.

- Opportunities and Threats: Globalization presents opportunities for companies to expand their markets and increase profitability. However, trade disputes, tariffs, and regulatory barriers can disrupt supply chains and impact corporate earnings.

- Adapting to Change: Investors need to be aware of the potential impact of geopolitical events on global markets. Staying informed about trade policies, tariffs, and international relations can help you anticipate market shifts and adjust your portfolio accordingly.

- Application: Monitor global trade developments and assess how they may impact your investments. Consider diversifying your portfolio across different regions and sectors to mitigate the risks associated with geopolitical uncertainties.

3. Demographic Shifts and Aging Populations

Demographic changes, such as aging populations in developed countries and youthful populations in emerging markets, are creating new investment opportunities and challenges. These shifts are influencing consumer behavior, labor markets, and economic growth patterns.

- Aging Populations: In countries with aging populations, such as Japan, Europe, and parts of North America, there is increasing demand for healthcare, retirement services, and products tailored to older adults. Companies that cater to these needs may experience significant growth.

- Youthful Populations: In contrast, emerging markets with youthful populations are experiencing rapid urbanization and rising consumer demand. These regions present opportunities in sectors such as education, technology, and consumer goods.

- Application: Consider demographic trends when making investment decisions. Allocate a portion of your portfolio to sectors that are likely to benefit from aging populations, such as healthcare and retirement services. Additionally, explore opportunities in emerging markets with youthful populations, particularly in industries poised for growth.

Conclusion: Embracing the Future of Investing

The future of minimalistic entrepreneurship and stock market investing is shaped by emerging trends that reflect broader changes in society, technology, and the global economy. By staying informed about the rise of ESG investing, the impact of artificial intelligence and big data, and the changing global economic landscapes, you can position yourself to capitalize on new opportunities while managing risks effectively.

As a Minimalistic Entrepreneur, embracing these trends requires a proactive approach to investing. It's about being open to new ideas, adapting to change, and continuously learning and evolving your strategy. By doing so, you can ensure that your investments remain aligned with your values, goals, and the realities of the modern world.

Remember, the key to success in the ever-changing world of investing is not just about following trends—it's about understanding how they fit into your overall financial plan and using them to enhance your journey toward financial freedom. Stay curious, stay informed, and stay committed to your goals, and you'll be well-equipped to navigate the future of minimalistic entrepreneurship with confidence and clarity.

Technology and Its Impact on Minimalistic Entrepreneurship

In the modern era, technology is not just a tool—it's a transformative force that is reshaping every aspect of our lives, including how we approach investing and entrepreneurship. For the Minimalistic Entrepreneur, technology offers unprecedented opportunities to streamline processes, make informed decisions, and access new markets and investment vehicles. By leveraging these technological advancements, you can enhance your efficiency, reduce costs, and stay ahead in an increasingly competitive landscape.

In this part, we'll explore the impact of technology on minimalistic entrepreneurship, focusing on three key areas: robo-advisors and algorithmic trading, blockchain and cryptocurrency considerations, and mobile investing and accessibility. By understanding these technological innovations and incorporating them into your strategy, you can optimize your approach to investing and entrepreneurship, ultimately accelerating your journey toward financial freedom.

Robo-Advisors and Algorithmic Trading: Automating Investment Management

The rise of robo-advisors and algorithmic trading has democratized access to sophisticated investment management tools that were once reserved for institutional investors. These technologies use algorithms and data-driven models to manage portfolios, execute trades, and optimize investment strategies—all with minimal human intervention. For the Minimalistic Entrepreneur, this means greater efficiency, lower costs, and the ability to focus on strategic decision-making rather than day-to-day management.

1. The Evolution of Robo-Advisors

Robo-advisors are automated platforms that use algorithms to create and manage investment portfolios based on an individual's risk tolerance, financial goals, and time horizon. These platforms offer a hands-off approach to investing, making them ideal for those who prefer simplicity and automation.

- Cost-Effective Portfolio Management: One of the most significant advantages of robo-advisors is their cost-effectiveness. Unlike traditional financial advisors who may charge substantial fees, robo-advisors typically offer lower management fees, making professional portfolio management accessible to a broader audience.

- Personalized Investment Strategies: Robo-advisors use sophisticated algorithms to design personalized investment strategies tailored to your specific needs. These strategies often involve diversified portfolios that are regularly rebalanced to maintain your desired asset allocation.

- Application: If you're looking to streamline your investment management process, consider using a robo-advisor. These platforms can handle everything from asset allocation to rebalancing, allowing you to focus on other aspects of your life and business. Popular robo-advisors like Betterment, Wealthfront, and Vanguard Personal Advisor Services offer a range of options depending on your financial goals and investment preferences.

2. The Role of Algorithmic Trading

Algorithmic trading, also known as algo-trading, involves the use of computer algorithms to execute trades at optimal prices and speeds. These algorithms analyze market data, identify trading opportunities, and execute orders based on pre-defined criteria, all within milliseconds. This technology has transformed the trading landscape, offering several benefits to investors.

- Speed and Efficiency: Algorithmic trading can execute trades much faster than any human trader, taking advantage of market inefficiencies and short-term opportunities. This speed can lead to better execution prices and reduced transaction costs.

- Data-Driven Decisions: Algorithms rely on vast amounts of data to make informed trading decisions. By analyzing historical data, market trends, and real-time information, algo-trading systems can optimize trade execution and reduce the impact of market fluctuations.

- Reducing Emotional Bias: One of the key advantages of algorithmic trading is its ability to remove emotional bias from the trading process. Since trades are executed based on pre-set criteria, there's no room for fear or greed to influence decisions, leading to more disciplined and consistent trading.

- Application: For more advanced investors, incorporating algorithmic trading into your strategy can provide a competitive edge. Whether through fully automated trading systems or using algo-trading strategies in conjunction with human oversight, this technology can enhance your ability to capitalize on market opportunities. Platforms like Interactive Brokers and TradeStation offer access to algorithmic trading tools that can be customized to fit your investment strategy.

Blockchain and Cryptocurrency Considerations: Navigating the Digital Frontier

Blockchain technology and cryptocurrencies represent one of the most disruptive forces in the financial industry. These innovations have the potential to revolutionize how we think about money, transactions, and even the concept of value itself. For the Minimalistic Entrepreneur, understanding the implications of blockchain and cryptocurrencies is essential for staying ahead in an increasingly digital world.

1. The Fundamentals of Blockchain Technology

At its core, blockchain is a decentralized, distributed ledger technology that records transactions across multiple computers in a way that is secure, transparent, and immutable. Each transaction is grouped into a block, and these blocks are linked together to form a chain—hence the term "blockchain."

- Security and Transparency: One of the key benefits of blockchain technology is its security. Because the ledger is decentralized and encrypted, it is highly resistant to tampering and fraud. Additionally, the transparency of blockchain allows anyone to verify transactions, fostering trust and accountability.

- Decentralization: Unlike traditional financial systems that rely on centralized authorities like banks or governments, blockchain operates on a peer-to-peer network. This decentralization reduces the risk of single points of failure and increases the resilience of the system.

- Application: As a Minimalistic Entrepreneur, it's important to understand how blockchain can impact your business and investments. Consider exploring blockchain-based applications beyond cryptocurrencies, such as smart contracts, decentralized finance (DeFi), and supply chain management solutions that leverage blockchain for greater efficiency and transparency.

2. Investing in Cryptocurrencies

Cryptocurrencies, such as Bitcoin, Ethereum, and many others, are digital or virtual currencies that use cryptography for security. They operate on blockchain technology and have gained significant attention as both an alternative form of money and a speculative investment.

- Volatility and Risk: Cryptocurrencies are known for their high volatility, which can lead to substantial gains but also significant losses. As a result, investing in cryptocurrencies requires a strong risk tolerance and a clear understanding of the market dynamics.

- Diversification and Allocation: For those interested in cryptocurrencies, it's crucial to approach them as part of a diversified portfolio. Given their volatility, it's advisable to allocate only a small portion of your overall portfolio to cryptocurrencies, balancing them with more traditional asset classes.

- Regulatory Considerations: The regulatory environment for cryptocurrencies is still evolving, and different countries have different approaches to regulation. Staying informed about the legal and regulatory landscape is essential for navigating potential risks and opportunities in the cryptocurrency market.

- Application: If you decide to invest in cryptocurrencies, start by educating yourself on the basics of blockchain and the specific cryptocurrencies you're interested in. Use reputable exchanges like Coinbase or Binance, and consider employing a secure wallet for storing your digital assets. Additionally, keep abreast of regulatory developments to ensure that your investments remain compliant with local laws.

3. The Potential of Decentralized Finance (DeFi)

Decentralized finance, or DeFi, is an emerging sector within the cryptocurrency space that aims to recreate traditional financial systems—such as lending, borrowing, trading, and insurance—using decentralized blockchain technology. DeFi platforms operate without intermediaries like banks, instead relying on smart contracts to automate financial transactions.

- Access and Inclusion: DeFi has the potential to democratize access to financial services, particularly for individuals in regions with limited access to traditional banking. By removing intermediaries, DeFi platforms can offer lower fees and greater accessibility to a global audience.

- Innovation and Yield Opportunities: DeFi platforms are at the forefront of financial innovation, offering unique opportunities for yield generation through staking, liquidity provision, and decentralized exchanges. However, these opportunities come with higher risks, including smart contract vulnerabilities and regulatory uncertainty.

- Application: For adventurous investors with a high risk tolerance, exploring DeFi could provide new opportunities for yield and portfolio diversification. Start by researching leading DeFi platforms like Uniswap, Aave, or Compound, and consider experimenting with small amounts of capital to understand how these systems work.

Mobile Investing and Accessibility: Empowering the Modern Investor

The advent of mobile investing has made the stock market more accessible than ever before. With the rise of smartphones and mobile apps, investors can now manage their portfolios, execute trades, and stay informed about market developments from virtually anywhere. This accessibility has leveled the playing field, allowing individuals from all walks of life to participate in the financial markets.

1. The Rise of Mobile Trading Platforms

Mobile trading platforms have revolutionized the way people invest by providing easy-to-use interfaces, real-time data, and low-cost trading options. These platforms empower investors to take control of their portfolios and make informed decisions on the go.

- User-Friendly Interfaces: Mobile trading apps are designed with simplicity in mind, making them accessible to both novice and experienced investors. Features like intuitive dashboards, customizable alerts, and one-click trading make it easier than ever to manage investments.

- Low-Cost Trading: Many mobile platforms, such as Robinhood, Zerodha, and eToro, offer commission-free trading or low fees, making it more affordable for individuals to buy and sell stocks, ETFs, and other assets. This democratization of trading has opened the doors for a new generation of investors.

- Application: If you're not already using a mobile trading app, consider downloading one that fits your investment style and preferences. These apps allow you to stay connected to the market, monitor your portfolio, and execute trades with ease, all from the convenience of your smartphone.

2. Accessibility and Financial Inclusion

Mobile investing has played a significant role in increasing financial inclusion, particularly in regions where traditional banking and investment services are less accessible. By providing access to global markets and financial tools, mobile platforms are empowering more people to build wealth and achieve financial independence.

- Global Reach: Mobile investing platforms are available to users across the globe, enabling individuals in developing countries to access international markets and diversify their portfolios. This global reach is helping to bridge the gap between emerging and developed markets.

- Educational Resources: Many mobile platforms offer educational resources, such as tutorials, articles, and videos, to help users learn about investing and improve their financial literacy. These resources are crucial for empowering new investors to make informed decisions.

- Application: Take advantage of the educational resources offered by mobile investing platforms to deepen your understanding of the markets and refine your investment strategy. Whether you're a beginner or an experienced investor, continuous learning is key to staying ahead in the ever-changing world of finance.

3. The Future of Mobile Investing

As technology continues to evolve, the future of mobile investing looks promising, with new features and innovations on the horizon. These advancements are likely to make investing even more accessible, personalized, and efficient.

- AI and Personalization: Future mobile platforms may incorporate more advanced AI-driven personalization, offering tailored investment advice, portfolio management, and financial planning based on an individual's unique circumstances and goals.

- Voice-Activated Trading: With the rise of voice-activated technology, it's possible that future mobile apps will allow users to execute trades and manage their portfolios using voice commands, further enhancing the convenience of mobile investing.

- Increased Integration with Other Financial Services: As mobile platforms continue to evolve, we may see greater integration with other financial services, such as banking, budgeting, and financial planning tools, creating a more comprehensive and seamless experience for users.

- Application: Stay informed about new developments in mobile investing technology and be open to adopting new tools and features that can enhance your investment experience. By embracing these innovations, you can continue to optimize your approach and stay ahead of the curve.

Conclusion: Embracing Technological Advancements in Minimalistic Entrepreneurship

Technology is a powerful enabler for the Minimalistic Entrepreneur, offering tools and platforms that can streamline your investment process, enhance your decision-making, and open up new opportunities. Whether it's leveraging robo-advisors for automated portfolio management, exploring the potential of blockchain and cryptocurrencies, or taking advantage of mobile investing to stay connected on the go, these technological advancements can significantly impact your journey toward financial freedom.

As you navigate the future of minimalistic entrepreneurship, it's essential to stay informed about emerging technologies and consider how they can be integrated into your overall strategy. By doing so, you'll be better equipped to capitalize on new opportunities, manage risks, and continue building a life of purpose, fulfillment, and financial independence.

Remember, the key to success in the digital age is not just adopting new technologies for the sake of it, but understanding how they can enhance your unique approach to entrepreneurship and investing. By staying curious, adaptable, and proactive, you can harness the power of technology to achieve your goals and thrive in an increasingly complex and interconnected world.

Adapting to Changing Market Conditions

In the ever-evolving landscape of the global economy, market conditions can change rapidly and unpredictably. As a Minimalistic Entrepreneur, your ability to adapt to these changes is crucial for maintaining and growing your investments. The key to thriving in varying market environments lies in staying informed about economic indicators, adjusting your strategies to match different market cycles, and preparing for potential market disruptions. By mastering these skills, you can safeguard your portfolio and continue progressing toward financial freedom, regardless of external economic forces.

In this part, we will delve into the strategies you need to stay ahead in a dynamic market. We will explore how to monitor and interpret economic indicators, how to adjust your investment strategies based on different market cycles, and how to prepare for potential market disruptions that could impact your financial well-being.

Staying Informed About Economic Indicators: The Compass for Navigating Markets

Economic indicators are critical tools that help investors understand the current state of the economy and anticipate future market trends. These indicators provide insights into economic growth, inflation, employment, and other factors that influence market conditions. By staying informed about these indicators, you can make more informed decisions and adjust your investment strategy accordingly.

1. Key Economic Indicators to Watch

Understanding which economic indicators to monitor is essential for navigating the markets. Some of the most influential indicators include:

- Gross Domestic Product (GDP): GDP measures the total value of goods and services produced in a country. It is a primary indicator of economic health. A growing GDP suggests a strong economy, while a declining GDP may signal a recession. Investors often look to GDP growth rates to gauge the overall direction of the economy.

- Inflation Rates: Inflation measures the rate at which prices for goods and services rise over time. Moderate inflation is a sign of a healthy economy, but high inflation can erode purchasing power and lead to tighter monetary policy. Central banks may raise interest rates to combat high inflation, which can impact stock and bond markets.

- Unemployment Rate: The unemployment rate indicates the percentage of the labor force that is unemployed and actively seeking work. A low unemployment rate generally reflects a strong labor market, which can boost consumer spending and economic growth. Conversely, a rising unemployment rate may indicate economic weakness.

- Consumer Confidence Index (CCI): The CCI measures the optimism or pessimism of consumers regarding their financial situation and the overall economy. High consumer confidence often correlates with increased spending and economic growth, while low confidence may signal reduced spending and potential economic slowdown.

- Interest Rates: Central banks, such as the Federal Reserve in the United States, set benchmark interest rates that influence borrowing costs and consumer behavior. Changes in interest rates can impact everything from mortgage rates to the cost of financing business operations, making them a crucial indicator for investors.

- Application: Regularly review economic reports and financial news to stay informed about these key indicators. Use them as a guide to assess the current economic climate and anticipate potential shifts in the market. Understanding these indicators will help you make more informed investment decisions and adjust your portfolio as needed.

2. Interpreting Economic Data for Investment Decisions

Interpreting economic data requires more than just understanding what each indicator means. It involves analyzing how different indicators interact with one another and considering the broader economic context.

- Correlations and Trends: Pay attention to how economic indicators move in relation to each other. For example, rising interest rates may coincide with a strengthening economy but could also lead to lower stock prices due to higher borrowing costs. Similarly, a strong GDP growth rate might be accompanied by rising inflation, prompting central banks to tighten monetary policy.

- Economic Cycles: The economy moves through cycles of expansion and contraction, and different economic indicators can signal where we are in the cycle. During an expansion, indicators like GDP and consumer confidence typically rise, while unemployment falls. In a contraction or recession, these trends may reverse.

- Application: Develop a habit of interpreting economic indicators within the context of broader economic cycles. This will allow you to anticipate shifts in the market and adjust your investment strategy to align with the current phase of the economic cycle.

3. Utilizing Economic Forecasts and Analysis

In addition to monitoring economic indicators, consider leveraging economic forecasts and analysis from reputable sources. Economists and financial analysts often provide insights into future economic conditions, helping investors make proactive adjustments to their strategies.

- Economic Forecasts: Many financial institutions and government agencies publish economic forecasts that project future trends in GDP, inflation, employment, and interest rates. These forecasts can provide valuable guidance for long-term investment planning.

- Market Analysis Reports: Financial news outlets and investment firms regularly publish market analysis reports that interpret recent economic data and offer insights into potential market movements. These reports can help you stay ahead of market trends and make informed decisions.

- Application: Subscribe to economic newsletters, follow financial news sources, and review reports from reputable analysts. Use this information to inform your investment decisions and stay proactive in adjusting your portfolio as market conditions change.

Adjusting Strategies for Different Market Cycles: Navigating the Ups and Downs

The stock market is cyclical, with periods of growth (bull markets) followed by periods of decline (bear markets). Adapting your investment strategy to different market cycles is essential for protecting your portfolio and maximizing returns. By understanding how to adjust your approach during various phases of the market cycle, you can navigate both good times and bad with confidence.

1. Strategies for Bull Markets

A bull market is characterized by rising stock prices, increasing investor confidence, and strong economic growth. During this phase, investors often experience significant gains, but it's important to remain vigilant and avoid becoming complacent.

- Growth-Oriented Investments: In a bull market, growth-oriented investments, such as stocks in high-growth sectors (technology, consumer discretionary), tend to outperform. Consider increasing your exposure to these sectors to take advantage of the market's upward momentum.

- Dollar-Cost Averaging: Even in a bull market, prices can be volatile. Dollar-cost averaging—investing a fixed amount at regular intervals—can help you avoid buying at market peaks and smooth out the cost of your investments over time.

- Rebalancing: As stock prices rise, your portfolio's asset allocation may drift from your target allocation, increasing your exposure to equities. Regularly rebalance your portfolio to maintain your desired risk level and prevent overexposure to any one asset class.

- Application: During a bull market, focus on growth investments but remain disciplined in your approach. Avoid chasing speculative gains and ensure that your portfolio remains diversified and aligned with your long-term goals.

2. Strategies for Bear Markets

A bear market is characterized by falling stock prices, declining investor confidence, and often economic contraction. While bear markets can be challenging, they also present opportunities for disciplined investors.

- Defensive Investments: In a bear market, consider shifting your portfolio towards defensive investments that are less sensitive to economic downturns. These may include sectors like utilities, consumer staples, and healthcare, which tend to perform better during market declines.

- Dividend Stocks: Dividend-paying stocks can provide a steady income stream during bear markets, helping to offset capital losses. Look for companies with strong balance sheets and a history of consistent dividend payments.

- Opportunistic Buying: Bear markets often lead to lower stock prices, presenting opportunities to buy high-quality stocks at a discount. If you have a long-term investment horizon, consider adding to your positions in fundamentally strong companies during market downturns.

- Application: In a bear market, prioritize capital preservation and focus on quality investments that can weather economic challenges. Stay patient and avoid panic selling—bear markets eventually give way to recovery, and disciplined investors can emerge stronger.

3. Preparing for Market Corrections and Volatility

Market corrections—typically defined as a decline of 10% or more in stock prices—are a normal part of the market cycle. While they can be unsettling, corrections often provide healthy rebalancing of overvalued markets and create buying opportunities for savvy investors.

- Maintaining Liquidity: Ensure that your portfolio has sufficient liquidity to take advantage of opportunities during market corrections. This might involve holding a portion of your portfolio in cash or short-term bonds that can be easily converted into equities when prices decline.

- Hedging Strategies: Consider using hedging strategies to protect your portfolio during periods of increased volatility. This could include investing in assets like gold, which historically perform well during market downturns, or using options to hedge against potential losses.

- Staying Disciplined: Volatile markets can test your resolve, but it's important to stay disciplined and stick to your long-term investment plan. Avoid making impulsive decisions based on short-term market movements, and remember that volatility is a normal part of investing.

- Application: During periods of market volatility, focus on maintaining a well-diversified portfolio, keeping liquidity for opportunistic buying, and using hedging strategies to mitigate risk. Stay calm and adhere to your long-term investment strategy, recognizing that volatility often precedes market recoveries.

Preparing for Potential Market Disruptions: Building Resilience

In today's interconnected world, markets are susceptible to disruptions from a wide range of sources, including geopolitical events, technological advancements, natural disasters, and pandemics. Building resilience into your investment strategy is essential for navigating these uncertainties and protecting your financial well-being.

1. Diversifying Across Asset Classes and Geographies

Diversification is one of the most effective ways to build resilience into your portfolio. By spreading your investments across different asset classes, sectors, and geographies, you can reduce the impact of any single event or market on your overall portfolio.

- Asset Class Diversification: Invest in a mix of asset classes, including stocks, bonds, real estate, and commodities. Different asset classes often respond differently to market disruptions, providing a buffer against losses in any one area.

- Geographic Diversification: Global events can impact markets differently depending on the region. By diversifying your investments across multiple geographies, you can reduce the risk associated with regional economic downturns or geopolitical tensions.

- Application: Regularly review your portfolio to ensure it is well-diversified across asset classes and geographies. Consider adding international stocks or funds to your portfolio to gain exposure to different markets and reduce concentration risk.

2. Building an Emergency Fund

An emergency fund is a critical component of financial resilience, providing a safety net in case of unexpected events such as job loss, medical emergencies, or market downturns. Having an emergency fund allows you to cover your expenses without needing to sell investments at a loss.

- Fund Size: Aim to build an emergency fund that covers at least three to six months' worth of living expenses. This fund should be kept in a highly liquid, low-risk account, such as a savings account or money market fund.

- Maintaining the Fund: Regularly contribute to your emergency fund, and avoid using it for non-emergencies. If you do need to tap into the fund, prioritize replenishing it as soon as possible.

- Application: Establish an emergency fund if you don't already have one, and treat it as a non-negotiable part of your financial plan. This fund will provide peace of mind and financial stability during times of uncertainty.

3. Stress Testing Your Portfolio

Stress testing involves evaluating how your portfolio would perform under different adverse scenarios, such as a recession, market crash, or interest rate hike. This process helps you identify potential vulnerabilities and make adjustments to strengthen your portfolio's resilience.

- Scenario Analysis: Conduct scenario analysis by modeling how your portfolio would react to various market conditions. Consider factors such as changes in interest rates, commodity prices, and currency fluctuations, and assess the potential impact on your investments.

- Adjusting for Risk: Based on the results of your stress tests, consider making adjustments to reduce risk, such as reallocating assets, increasing diversification, or adding hedging strategies.

- Application: Periodically stress test your portfolio to ensure it is well-positioned to withstand market disruptions. Use the insights gained from this analysis to make informed adjustments that enhance your portfolio's resilience.

Conclusion: Thriving in a Changing Market

Adapting to changing market conditions is a fundamental skill for the Minimalistic Entrepreneur. By staying informed about economic indicators, adjusting your strategies to match different market cycles, and preparing for potential market disruptions, you can build a resilient investment portfolio that thrives in both good times and bad.

Remember, the key to successful investing is not just about picking the right stocks or timing the market—it's about staying flexible, informed, and disciplined in the face of uncertainty. By embracing these principles, you can navigate the complexities of the global economy, protect your financial future, and continue your journey toward financial freedom with confidence and clarity.

As you move forward, keep in mind that markets will always experience cycles of growth and decline, and disruptions are inevitable. However, with the right mindset and strategies, you can turn challenges into opportunities, build wealth, and achieve your long-term goals, no matter what the future holds.

CHAPTER TWELVE

THE PRINCIPLES OF THE MINIMALISTIC ENTREPRENEUR

In the intricate world of investing, where opportunities are abundant but so are the risks, success often hinges not on how much you do, but on how well you do it. This is the essence of minimalistic entrepreneurship—a strategic approach that emphasizes clarity, focus, and purpose in every decision. As a minimalistic entrepreneur, your goal is to maximize impact while minimizing complexity, ensuring that each action you take is deliberate and aligned with your long-term financial objectives.

Guiding this approach are a set of principles that serve as the foundation for your investment strategy. These principles are not just abstract concepts; they are practical guidelines that shape your decision-making process, helping you navigate the financial landscape with confidence and discipline. In this chapter, we will explore the core principles of the minimalistic entrepreneur and how they can be applied to create a successful and sustainable investment strategy.

Why Principles Matter:

Every successful investor or entrepreneur has a set of guiding principles—rules or beliefs that steer their decisions and actions. For the minimalistic entrepreneur, these principles are crucial because they provide a framework for making informed, consistent decisions, even in the face of market volatility or uncertainty. By adhering to these principles, you can avoid the pitfalls of impulsive decision-making, stay focused on your long-term goals, and ultimately, achieve financial independence.

Section 1: Principle of Strategic Simplicity

Defining Strategic Simplicity:

Strategic simplicity is the cornerstone of minimalistic entrepreneurship. It's the practice of focusing on what truly matters—selecting high-impact actions that drive growth and eliminating distractions that add unnecessary complexity. In the realm of investing, this means concentrating on a few well-chosen investments that align with your financial goals rather than diversifying excessively and diluting your efforts.

Strategic simplicity is about making deliberate choices. It's about recognizing that not all opportunities are worth pursuing and that sometimes, doing less can lead to more significant results. This principle encourages you to streamline your portfolio, focus on quality over quantity, and ensure that each investment serves a clear, defined purpose within your broader strategy.

Applying Strategic Simplicity in Investing:

- Streamlined Portfolio:

Building a streamlined portfolio is a fundamental aspect of strategic simplicity. This involves carefully selecting a limited number of high-quality assets that align with your financial objectives. Rather than spreading your investments across numerous assets, you focus on those with the strongest potential for long-term growth and stability. This approach not only simplifies portfolio management but also enhances your ability to monitor and adjust your investments effectively.

- Clear Investment Criteria:

Establishing clear investment criteria is another critical component of strategic simplicity. Before making any investment, you should have a set of specific, well-defined criteria that each asset must meet. This could include factors such as the asset's risk level, potential return, alignment with your financial goals, and fit within your overall portfolio. By adhering to these criteria, you ensure that every investment decision is purposeful and contributes to your long-term strategy.

Case Study:

Consider the case of an investor who embodies strategic simplicity. This investor, recognizing the value of focus, built a portfolio around a core group of blue-chip stocks—companies with strong fundamentals, consistent dividends, and a history of stability. Rather than chasing high-risk, high-reward opportunities, the investor stuck to their criteria, selecting only those stocks that met their stringent requirements. Over time, this disciplined approach paid off, resulting in steady, reliable returns and a portfolio that weathered market fluctuations with resilience.

Section 2: Principle of Intentionality

The Power of Purposeful Investing:

Intentionality is about making every decision with purpose. In the context of investing, it means that each action you take should be deliberate and aligned with your long-term goals. The principle of intentionality ensures that you invest not out of impulse or fear of missing out, but because the investment serves a specific, meaningful purpose within your overall strategy.

Purposeful investing is the antithesis of speculative investing. It's not about taking chances on the latest market trend or hot stock tip. Instead, it's about being methodical and disciplined, ensuring that every investment decision is backed by thorough research and a clear understanding of how it fits into your financial plan.

Aligning Investments with Goals:

- Goal-Oriented Portfolio Construction:

To apply the principle of intentionality, start by defining your core financial goals. Are you investing for retirement, to generate passive income, or to preserve wealth? Once your goals are clear, you can construct a portfolio that is tailored to achieving them. Each asset you add to your portfolio should have a specific role in helping you reach your objectives, whether it's providing growth, generating income, or offering stability.

- Avoiding Fads and Trends:

One of the greatest challenges in investing is resisting the temptation to chase market trends or fads. Intentionality requires you to stay focused on your strategy, even when others are jumping on the latest bandwagon. By sticking to your long-term goals and investment criteria, you can avoid the risks associated with speculative investing and maintain a portfolio that is stable, balanced, and aligned with your objectives.

Practical Exercise:

Take a moment to reflect on your current portfolio. Does each investment align with your core financial goals? If not, consider how you can adjust your portfolio to better reflect your intentions. Create a list of your top three financial goals and evaluate whether your current investments support them. This exercise will help you bring intentionality into your investing process, ensuring that every decision is purpose-driven and aligned with your long-term strategy.

Section 3: Principle of Patience and Discipline

Long-Term Perspective:

Patience is a virtue, especially in investing. The principle of patience and discipline is about maintaining a long-term perspective, recognizing that true wealth is built over time, not overnight. As a minimalistic entrepreneur, you understand that market fluctuations are inevitable, but your focus remains on the bigger picture—achieving your long-term financial goals through steady, consistent growth.

Patience requires the ability to stay the course, even when markets are volatile or when the media is filled with doom-and-gloom predictions. It's about trusting your strategy and resisting the urge to make knee-jerk reactions to short-term market movements.

Staying Disciplined in Volatile Markets:

- Emotional Control:

Emotions can be a significant obstacle to successful investing. Fear, greed, and anxiety often lead to impulsive decisions that can derail your long-term strategy. To maintain discipline, it's essential to manage these emotions and make decisions based on logic and reason, not on how you feel at the moment. Techniques such as setting predefined rules for buying and selling or automating your investments can help remove emotion from the equation.

- Consistent Review and Rebalancing:

Discipline also involves regularly reviewing and rebalancing your portfolio to ensure it remains aligned with your goals. This doesn't mean constantly tweaking your investments in response to every market movement, but rather, making thoughtful adjustments when necessary. By staying disciplined in your approach, you can ensure that your portfolio continues to reflect your long-term strategy, even as market conditions change.

Case Study:

Consider an investor who remained disciplined during a significant market downturn. While others panicked and sold their assets at a loss, this investor held steady, trusting in their long-term strategy. They had built a diversified portfolio that was designed to withstand market volatility, and rather than reacting impulsively, they used the downturn as an opportunity to rebalance their portfolio and buy high-quality assets at lower prices. In the long run, this disciplined approach resulted in significant gains, reinforcing the importance of patience and discipline in investing.

Section 4: Principle of Focused Growth

Quality Over Quantity:

In the pursuit of growth, it's easy to fall into the trap of trying to do too much—investing in too many assets, chasing too many opportunities. However, the principle of focused growth emphasizes the importance of quality over quantity. As a minimalistic entrepreneur, your goal is to concentrate your resources on high-quality investments that offer strong growth potential, rather than spreading yourself too thin.

Focused growth means identifying the areas where you can achieve the greatest impact and dedicating your efforts to those areas. It's about being selective, choosing only the investments that truly align with your financial goals and that have the potential to deliver the results you seek.

Concentrated Investing:

- Building a Focused Portfolio:

A focused portfolio is one that is carefully constructed to include only those assets that you believe in fully. This might mean concentrating on a few select stocks, sectors, or asset classes that you know well and have thoroughly researched. While this approach can increase risk, it also allows you to deepen your knowledge of your investments and make more informed decisions.

- Managing Risk in a Concentrated Portfolio:

While focused investing can lead to significant gains, it's important to manage the risks associated with concentration. This might involve diversifying within your chosen area of focus, using risk management strategies such as stop-loss orders, or maintaining a core of more stable investments to balance out the higher risk of your focused assets.

Practical Exercise:

Examine your current portfolio and identify your top-performing assets. Consider whether there are opportunities to focus more on these areas, perhaps by increasing your allocation to these assets or by further researching related opportunities. At the same time, evaluate the risks associated with concentrating your investments and develop a plan to manage those risks effectively.

Section 5: Principle of Continuous Learning and Adaptation

The Importance of Ongoing Education:

The financial markets are dynamic, constantly evolving in response to economic developments, technological advancements, and global events. As a minimalistic entrepreneur, it's crucial to commit to continuous learning, ensuring that you stay informed and adaptable in the face of change. The principle of continuous learning and adaptation emphasizes the need for ongoing education and the ability to adjust your strategy as needed.

Ongoing education means staying curious, seeking out new knowledge, and remaining open to new ideas. It's about understanding that the investment strategies that worked yesterday may not be as effective tomorrow, and that staying ahead of the curve requires a commitment to lifelong learning.

Adapting to Market Changes:

- Staying Ahead of Trends:

The financial landscape is shaped by trends that can create both opportunities and risks. Whether it's the rise of new technologies, shifts in global markets, or changes in consumer behavior, being able to recognize and respond to these trends is critical. This doesn't mean chasing every new development, but rather, staying informed and being prepared to adjust your strategy when necessary.

- Learning from Mistakes:

Every investor makes mistakes, but the key to long-term success is learning from those mistakes and applying those lessons to future decisions. Reflecting on past decisions, understanding what went wrong, and identifying how you can improve is a crucial part of the minimalistic entrepreneur's journey.

Action Plan:

To put this principle into practice, create a personal learning plan that includes regular updates on market trends, new investment opportunities, and reviews of your past decisions. Identify resources that can help you stay informed, such as financial news outlets, investment books, or online courses. By committing to continuous learning and adaptation, you ensure that your investment strategy remains relevant, effective, and aligned with your long-term goals.

Conclusion: Embracing the Minimalistic Entrepreneurial Mindset

Recap of Core Principles:

The principles of minimalistic entrepreneurship—strategic simplicity, intentionality, patience and discipline, focused growth, and continuous learning and adaptation—form the foundation of a successful investment strategy. Together, these principles guide you in making informed, deliberate decisions that maximize impact while minimizing complexity. They help you stay focused on your long-term goals, maintain discipline in the face of market volatility, and continuously improve your strategy over time.

As you continue on your journey as a minimalistic entrepreneur, I encourage you to actively apply these principles to your investing process. Remember, minimalism in entrepreneurship isn't just about doing less—it's about doing what matters most, with intention, focus, and discipline. By adhering to these principles, you can build a portfolio that is not only resilient and successful but also aligned with your personal values and long-term financial goals.

Final Thoughts:

Embracing the principles of minimalistic entrepreneurship can lead to a more fulfilling and successful approach to investing. It's about finding clarity in complexity, making purposeful decisions, and achieving your financial goals with intention and focus. As you apply these principles, you'll discover that less truly is more—more impact, more success, and more fulfillment in your journey to financial independence.

Conclusion

As we reach the conclusion of this journey, it's time to reflect on the core principles of minimalistic entrepreneurship and how they can guide you toward a life of financial independence, reduced stress, and lasting satisfaction. The Minimalistic Entrepreneur approach is more than just a strategy for managing investments—it's a philosophy for living a purposeful and balanced life, where your financial goals are aligned with your personal values and long-term aspirations.

In conclusion, we will recap the key principles that have shaped this approach, outline actionable steps for starting your journey, and explore the profound benefits of embracing minimalistic entrepreneurship in the long term. By internalizing these concepts and applying them to your life, you can create a future that not only meets your financial goals but also enhances your overall well-being and leaves a meaningful legacy.

Recap of Key Principles

Summary of Minimalistic Entrepreneurship Philosophy

At its core, minimalistic entrepreneurship is about simplifying your financial and personal life to focus on what truly matters. It's a philosophy that emphasizes quality over quantity, intentional living, and making thoughtful decisions that align with your values and long-term goals. The minimalistic entrepreneur does not chase after every opportunity or clutter their life with unnecessary distractions. Instead, they cultivate a mindset of abundance through simplicity, investing in assets that grow over time and contribute to a life of freedom and fulfillment.

- Intentional Living:

Minimalistic entrepreneurship is rooted in the belief that less is often more. By focusing on what is essential and eliminating the superfluous, you create space for growth, creativity, and meaningful experiences. This applies not only to your financial decisions but also to how you spend your time, energy, and resources.

- *Value-Driven Investing:*

Rather than seeking quick profits or following the latest trends, the minimalistic entrepreneur invests with purpose. This means prioritizing investments that align with your values, have long-term growth potential, and contribute to your overall financial independence. It's about making decisions that reflect your personal goals and ethics, ensuring that your financial success is sustainable and meaningful.

- *Simplicity and Clarity:*

The minimalistic approach favors simplicity in both strategy and execution. Whether it's automating your investments, streamlining your portfolio, or focusing on a few key financial goals, simplicity leads to clarity and reduces the risk of overwhelm. This clarity allows you to make more informed decisions and stay committed to your long-term plan.

Review of Essential Investing Strategies

Throughout this book, we've explored various investing strategies that are integral to the minimalistic entrepreneur approach. These strategies are designed to help you build wealth steadily and sustainably while minimizing unnecessary risk and complexity.

- *Diversification:*

Diversification is a cornerstone of smart investing, helping to spread risk across different asset classes, sectors, and geographies. By diversifying your portfolio, you reduce the impact of any single investment's performance on your overall wealth, creating a more resilient financial foundation.

- *Long-Term Investing:*

Patience is key to the minimalistic entrepreneur's success. Long-term investing involves holding onto investments through market cycles, avoiding the temptation to make short-term trades based on market fluctuations. This strategy allows you to benefit from the compounding effect and the general upward trajectory of the markets over time.

- *Rebalancing and Regular Review:*

Regularly rebalancing your portfolio ensures that it remains aligned with your risk tolerance and financial goals. It's important to periodically review your investments, making adjustments as needed to stay on track and capitalize on opportunities that align with your long-term strategy.

- *Risk Management:*

Managing risk is about understanding your own risk tolerance and making investment decisions that reflect it. This includes maintaining an emergency fund, avoiding overexposure to volatile assets, and being prepared for market downturns. By managing risk effectively, you protect your portfolio from significant losses and ensure steady progress toward your financial goals.

The Importance of Patience and Long-Term Thinking

Patience and long-term thinking are the bedrock of the minimalistic entrepreneur approach. In a world that often prioritizes instant gratification, the ability to think and act with a long-term perspective sets you apart. This mindset allows you to stay focused on your goals, even when faced with short-term challenges or market volatility.

- *Delayed Gratification:*

Financial success through minimalistic entrepreneurship often involves delaying immediate rewards in favor of long-term benefits. This means choosing to invest in your future rather than spending impulsively, and recognizing that the most meaningful rewards come from sustained effort over time.

- *Consistency and Discipline:*

Consistent, disciplined investing—whether through regular contributions, reinvesting dividends, or sticking to your long-term strategy—is what ultimately drives success. The minimalistic entrepreneur knows that wealth is built over decades, not days, and that staying the course is often the most effective strategy.

- *Trust in the Process:*

Long-term thinking requires trust in the process. Markets will fluctuate, and there will be periods of uncertainty, but by maintaining a long-term focus, you position yourself to benefit from the natural growth of the economy and the power of compounding. Trusting the process means resisting the urge to make reactive decisions based on short-term events.

Taking the First Steps on Your Minimalistic Entrepreneur Journey

Action Plan for Getting Started

Embarking on your journey as a minimalistic entrepreneur starts with taking actionable steps that align with the principles outlined in this book. Here's a step-by-step guide to help you get started:

- Assess Your Current Situation: Begin by evaluating your current financial situation. Take stock of your assets, liabilities, income, and expenses. Understanding where you stand today is crucial for setting realistic goals and creating a plan to achieve them.

- Define Your Financial Goals: Clearly define your short-term and long-term financial goals. These goals should be specific, measurable, achievable, relevant, and time-bound (SMART). Whether it's saving for retirement, buying a home, or achieving financial independence, your goals will guide your investment strategy and decision-making.

- Simplify Your Financial Life: Look for ways to simplify your financial life. This might involve consolidating accounts, automating savings and investments, and reducing unnecessary expenses. Simplification reduces stress and allows you to focus on what truly matters.

- Create a Diversified Investment Portfolio: Based on your goals and risk tolerance, create a diversified investment portfolio that includes a mix of asset classes such as stocks, bonds, and real estate. Diversification helps manage risk and ensures that your portfolio is well-balanced.

- Commit to Regular Investing: Establish a habit of regular investing, whether through a systematic investment plan (SIP) or by setting aside a fixed percentage of your income each month. Consistency is key to building wealth over time.

- Monitor and Adjust: Regularly review your progress toward your goals and make adjustments as needed. This includes rebalancing your portfolio, revisiting your financial plan, and staying informed about changes in the market and economy.

Setting Realistic Expectations

Setting realistic expectations is essential for staying motivated and avoiding disappointment. Understand that building wealth through minimalistic entrepreneurship is a gradual process that requires time, patience, and discipline.

- Time Horizon: Recognize that financial goals, especially long-term ones like retirement or financial independence, take years or even decades to achieve. Be patient and stay focused on the long-term benefits of your strategy.

- Market Volatility: Expect that the markets will fluctuate. There will be periods of growth and periods of decline, but over the long term, markets tend to trend upward. By maintaining a long-term perspective, you can weather short-term volatility without losing sight of your goals.

- Progress, Not Perfection: Understand that progress is not always linear. There will be setbacks, but the key is to keep moving forward. Celebrate your achievements along the way and learn from any challenges you encounter.

Overcoming Common Obstacles

As you embark on your minimalistic entrepreneur journey, you may encounter obstacles that challenge your resolve. Being prepared for these challenges will help you stay on track.

- Emotional Decision-Making: One of the biggest challenges in investing is managing emotions, especially during market downturns. Avoid making impulsive decisions based on fear or greed. Instead, rely on your long-term plan and stay disciplined in your approach.

- Information Overload: With the vast amount of financial information available today, it's easy to feel overwhelmed. Focus on the essentials and filter out noise. Stick to your strategy and avoid chasing after the latest trends or market fads.

- Impatience: The desire for quick results can lead to impatience and short-term thinking. Remind yourself that true financial success is built over time. Stay committed to your long-term goals and trust in the process.

- External Pressures: You may face external pressures from friends, family, or the media to make certain financial decisions. Remember that your financial journey is unique to you. Make decisions based on your values, goals, and circumstances, not on the opinions of others.

The Long-Term Benefits of the Minimalistic Entrepreneur Approach

Financial Independence and Freedom

The ultimate goal of minimalistic entrepreneurship is financial independence—the point at which your passive income and investments are sufficient to cover your living expenses, allowing you to live life on your own terms. Achieving financial independence provides you with the freedom to pursue your passions, spend time with loved ones, and live a life that aligns with your values.

- Freedom from Financial Stress: Financial independence eliminates the stress of living paycheck to paycheck or worrying about unexpected expenses. It provides a sense of security and peace of mind, knowing that you have the resources to weather any financial storm.

- Pursuing Passions: With financial independence, you have the freedom to pursue activities that bring you joy and fulfillment, whether that's starting a business, traveling the world, or dedicating time to hobbies and creative pursuits.

- Living with Purpose: Financial independence allows you to focus on what truly matters to you. It gives you the time and resources to make a positive impact in the world, whether through philanthropy, volunteering, or simply living a life that reflects your values.

Reduced Stress and Increased Life Satisfaction

One of the most significant benefits of the minimalistic entrepreneur approach is the reduction in stress and the increase in overall life satisfaction. By simplifying your financial life and focusing on long-term goals, you can create a more balanced and fulfilling lifestyle.

- Simplified Finances: A minimalist approach to your finances reduces the complexity and confusion that often leads to stress. By automating investments, reducing expenses, and focusing on essential financial goals, you create a more manageable and stress-free financial plan.

- Work-Life Balance: Financial independence provides the flexibility to achieve a better work-life balance. You can choose to work less, spend more time with family, or pursue personal interests without the pressure of financial obligations.

- Contentment and Fulfillment: Minimalistic entrepreneurship encourages you to find contentment in what you have, rather than constantly striving for more. This mindset shift leads to greater satisfaction with life and a deeper sense of fulfillment.

Creating a Lasting Legacy

The impact of your financial decisions extends beyond your own life. By embracing minimalistic entrepreneurship, you have the opportunity to create a lasting legacy for future generations.

- Generational Wealth: Through disciplined investing and thoughtful financial planning, you can build generational wealth that provides for your family and future descendants. This wealth can support their education, health, and well-being, giving them a solid foundation for their own lives.

- Philanthropy and Giving Back: Financial independence allows you to give back to causes and communities that matter to you. Whether through charitable donations, establishing a foundation, or volunteering your time, you can make a meaningful difference in the world.

- Inspiring Others: By living as a Minimalistic Entrepreneur, you inspire others to pursue financial independence and live a life aligned with their values. Your journey can serve as a model for those around you, encouraging them to take control of their finances and create their own path to success.

Conclusion: A Life Well-Lived

The Minimalistic Entrepreneur approach is more than just a financial strategy—it's a way of life. It's about making intentional choices, focusing on what truly matters, and building a future that reflects your values and goals. By embracing this approach, you can achieve financial independence, reduce stress, and live a life of purpose, fulfillment, and lasting impact.

As you move forward on your journey, remember that the path to financial freedom is not always easy, but it is incredibly rewarding. Stay committed to your goals, remain patient and disciplined, and trust in the process. With time, effort, and the right mindset, you can create a life that is not only financially secure but also rich in meaning and satisfaction.

This is the essence of the Minimalistic Entrepreneur approach—a life well-lived, where financial success is not an end in itself but a means to a greater purpose. Embrace this philosophy, take the first steps on your journey, and enjoy the many rewards that come with living as a Minimalistic Entrepreneur.